THE WISCONSIN HISTORICAL SOCIETY

The

WISCONSIN
HISTORICAL
SOCIETY

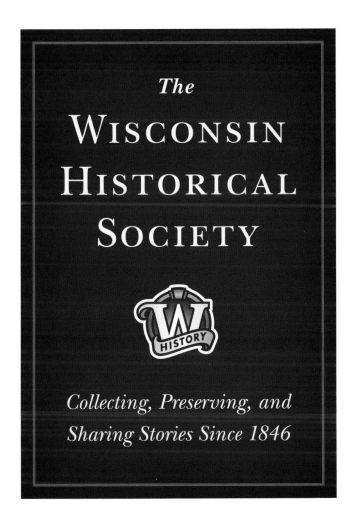

*Collecting, Preserving, and
Sharing Stories Since 1846*

JOHN ZIMM

The Wisconsin Historical Society Press

Published by the Wisconsin Historical Society Press
Publishers since 1855

© 2015 by the State Historical Society of Wisconsin

For permission to reuse material from *The Wisconsin Historical Society*, 978-0-87020-691-7, please access www.copyright.com or contact the Copyright Clearance Center, Inc. (CCC), 222 Rosewood Drive, Danvers, MA 01923, 978-750-8400. CCC is a not-for-profit organization that provides licenses and registration for a variety of users.

wisconsin**history**.org

Printed in Wisconsin, USA, on Wisconsin-made paper

18   17   16   15   14   1   2   3   4   5

Library of Congress Cataloging-in-Publication Data
Zimm, John.
    The Wisconsin Historical Society : collecting, preserving and sharing stories since 1846 / John Zimm.
        pages cm
    Includes bibliographical references and index.
    ISBN 978-0-87020-691-7 (hardcover : alk. paper) — ISBN 978-0-87020-692-4 (ebook) 1. Wisconsin Historical Society. 2. Wisconsin—History. 3. Historic preservation—Wisconsin. I. Title.
    F576.Z55 2014
    977.5—dc23

                                                                                    2014043915

♾ The paper used in this publication meets the t requirements of the American National Standard for Information Sciences—Permanence of Paper for Printed Library Materials, ANSI Z39.48-1992.

*To all those who have worked to treasure up
Wisconsin's past for future generations*

CONTENTS

1 *Introduction*
HISTORY TREASURED UP

3 *Chapter 1*
"EXPLOITS, PERILS AND HARDY
ADVENTURES": THE EARLY YEARS

21 *Chapter 2*
THE GOLDEN AGE

39 *Chapter 3*
DOOMSDAY

51 *Chapter 4*
LORD'S WAY

71 *Chapter 5*
THE GRAND OLD LADY'S NEW ERA

95 *Chapter 6*
MODERN TIMES

123 *Conclusion*
A SOLEMN TRUST

125 *Acknowledgments*
127 *List of Society Directors*
129 *List of Images*
133 *Notes*
141 *Index*

Editor's Note

The following pages bring to life many of the people and events that helped the Wisconsin Historical Society become the leading historical agency it is today, preserving and sharing the rich stories of our state and nation so that our future may be informed by our past. While the legal name of the organization is the State Historical Society of Wisconsin, since 2001 it has been known as the Wisconsin Historical Society. For the sake of clarity and consistency, we've made the decision to refer to ourselves throughout this book as "Wisconsin Historical Society" or simply "the Society."

Introduction

HISTORY
TREASURED UP

In the autumn of 1845, two Wisconsin pioneers happened upon each other. One of them, Richard Magoon, was an early settler of Lafayette County and a Black Hawk War veteran. The other, Chauncey Britt, was the editor of the Mineral Point *Democrat.* The two men were living in rapidly changing times, and Magoon worried about losing the history of the territory he had helped to settle. Magoon suggested to Britt that someone should organize "an Historical Society, to collect, from the pioneers then alive, such facts in regard to the early history of Wisconsin, as they might possess, as well as to treasure up those occurring in the future."[1]

Chauncey Britt agreed. He printed an unassuming article in the *Democrat* calling for help from his "brethren of the press."[2]

"There are hundreds of men now in Wisconsin who could furnish much valuable information relative to the early history of the Territory," Britt wrote. "A few years more, and they will have passed away, and the future people of Wisconsin will seek in vain for the information which they can now communicate."[3]

Magoon's suggestion, and Britt's forward-looking appeal, set in motion the creation of one of the largest, most active, and most diversified state historical societies in the nation: the Wisconsin Historical Society, older by two years than the state itself. Today, the Society boasts an extraordinary Library and Archival holdings, available to Wisconsinites and researchers from around the world; manages eleven Historic Sites and the flagship Wisconsin Historical Museum; guides a network of almost four hundred local historical societies; and actively preserves historically and archaeologically important places across our grand state.

Image of the Eben Peck cabin, painted by Isabella Dengel in 1891. Built in 1837, the Peck cabin was the first building in Madison, the city where only nine years later the Wisconsin Historical Society would be founded.

From its start, the Society has been a pioneer among other historical institutions, with a unique relationship to the people of Wisconsin. In 1854, the Wisconsin Historical Society became the first in the country to receive government funding. As a uniquely public institution, the Society's leaders understood their responsibility to "treasure up" the stories of people from all walks of life. This emphasis on our state's social history has enriched our knowledge of the past through the preservation of stories that include women, American Indians, African Americans, laborers, and many others whose voices are traditionally ignored. The Society preserves and shares the stories and objects of people from every corner of the state. Membership is open to all who pay annual dues, and the Society's collections belong to the people of Wisconsin.

Unlikely as it may have seemed, all of this began in a frontier territory with no railroads, in a capital city with dirt streets, where wolves and prairie fires were still hazards—in short, a place where history seemed more to be made rather than preserved. The creation of the Wisconsin Historical Society is a manifold tale of pioneers, perseverance, and forward-looking vision.

Chapter One

"EXPLOITS, PERILS AND HARDY ADVENTURES": THE EARLY YEARS

1846–1880s

Chauncey Britt printed a second entreaty in September 1846, this time in the pages of the Milwaukee *Courier*. At the time, delegates from around Wisconsin were preparing to gather in Madison for the territory's first constitutional convention. Britt's appeal captured the delegates' attention. Quietly, several delegates gathered for a series of meetings, first at Morrison's American Hotel on the Capitol Square and later at the library in Wisconsin's capitol building. We don't know much about these meetings; the notes vanished with an attendee who moved to California soon after and promptly died. Yet, that fall, the state delegates created a basic organizational structure for a state Historical Society and elected officers. Among them were prominent men of the territory, including noted scientist Increase Lapham, businessmen Solomon Juneau and Byron Kilbourn, banker Samuel Marshall, and former territorial governor James Duane Doty.

In January 1847, the officers gathered in Madison for the first annual meeting of the Wisconsin Historical Society. That meeting was representative of the early years of the organization. Former governor Doty, one of the Society's vice presidents, was selected to

Some of the first officers of the Wisconsin Historical Society.
Clockwise from top left: Solomon Juneau, Byron Kilbourn,
Samuel Marshall, and James Duane Doty

speak before the assembled crowd, but he did not. Officers were
elected to serve for the following year, but otherwise there was little
activity. As one participant recounted, "I do not think much was
done other than making an organization."

In January 1849, members reorganized the Society with the
aim of creating a more active organization. They adopted a constitution establishing the purpose of the Society to "preserve the
materials for a complete history of Wisconsin embracing the antiquities, and the history of the Indian tribes."[1] Attendees also

Increase Lapham, one of Wisconsin's most noteworthy scientists, was one of the charter members and cofounders of the Wisconsin Historical Society. Lapham's many accomplishments include writing a pioneering work in 1867 on the destruction of forests, helping establish the Milwaukee public high school program, and helping create the National Weather Bureau, the forerunner of today's National Weather Service.

adopted several resolutions. One of them was a request by Increase Lapham, future state geologist and father of the United States Weather Bureau, that "surveyors throughout this state be requested to furnish this Society with sketches from actual measurements of the ancient mounds and artificial earth-works in their vicinity."[2] The Society elected Governor Nelson Dewey its president, while designating the bright and ambitious Lapham corresponding secretary. The Society began with the daunting task of accumulating a library, starting with the *Laws* and *Journals* of the Wisconsin Territory, as well as government documents from New York State and the Smithsonian Institution.

Over the next three years, Society members met each year in the Governor's Room of the state capitol to elect officers and listen to an address. The Society admitted new members to the fold and raised money through annual membership dues, which stood at fifty cents in 1849. The Society was led by a three-member executive committee, and it had twenty-five vice presidents, one from each county. Additionally, the Society had a treasurer, a recording secretary, and a corresponding secretary whose position would evolve to be comparable to today's director.[3] Still, the Society accomplished little else. In 1852, the Library numbered fifty volumes, just enough to fill a cabinet in the corner of the Governor's Room. Though various members made plans and sought financial support to write a history of Wisconsin, little ink was spilled to fulfill this ambition.

Then, in 1852, Lyman Draper arrived on the scene. Thanks to Draper's innovations, the Society would soon be the envy of many more established East Coast institutions.

Lyman Draper: A Small Man with Big Ideas

Lyman Copeland Draper was born on September 4, 1815, in Erie County, New York, on a farm at the mouth of Eighteen Mile Creek, so named because it was eighteen miles from Buffalo.[4] Lyman's father, Luke Draper, was a restless man, a sometimes tavern keeper, and a farmer who had a keen interest in medicine. Luke moved his family several times, seeking different opportunities along the eastern shore of Lake Erie, before settling in Lockport, New York, in 1821.[5]

Luke kept a tavern in Lockport, where young Lyman heard accounts from his father's patrons of adventure and war on the western frontier. Lyman also absorbed the stories of his grandfather Jonathan Draper, who had been one of the minutemen at Lexington during the Revolutionary War and who later did sporadic duty in the New Hampshire militia, combating British raiding parties.[6] Lyman's father was also a veteran, having seen occasional service in the War of 1812 as it played out on New York's western frontier. Luke Draper was captured by the British, came under cannon fire while sailing with a couple of companions, and served with the New York militia that was disbanded rather than used to defend Fort George. On his way home from Fort George, Luke and another man were captured again by the British and hauled to Montreal for imprisonment.

As he grew, young Lyman listened to these tales of high adventure and lamented the fact that he did not find accounts such as these in the books he read or in the words of the orators. In time,

Lyman would resolve to remedy this neglect and save from oblivion the stories of lesser-known men who, in Lyman's words, "suffered more, and were honored less, than almost any equal number of adventurers in any country or age."[7]

Lyman inherited his mother Harriet's diminutive frame, growing to only five feet tall and one hundred pounds, hardly bigger than a schoolboy. "I am a small bit of a fellow," he would one day explain.[8] A correspondent later joked that Draper could "jump into one of my pockets and [I'll] carry you all over the plantation . . . taking care you don't fall out and

Lyman Draper directed the Society for more than three decades, during which he built notable Library and manuscript collections and assembled the Museum, or "Cabinet" as it was then called.

break your neck."[9] His younger brothers quickly grew larger and more robust, and the restlessness and vigor he inherited from his father were directed toward the mind and the imagination. Draper read voraciously, did well in the intermittent schooling he received as a youth, and won the respect of the locals in Lockport through his learnedness.[10]

At age seventeen, Draper began trying his hand at writing, showing even at that age an unusual devotion to accuracy. Yet writing seemed to afflict the fragile little man with an odd array of ailments.[11] As he matured and his ambitions grew, Draper planned to write a magnificent series of biographies of the pioneers, but these works would go mostly unwritten as hypochondria got the better of him. Time and again he postponed his writing to collect more material or to treat a variety of maladies. Ultimately, Draper would complete very few works of his own; it is as a collector that he is remembered.

As a teenager in the 1830s, Draper began corresponding with pioneers and their descendants, a lifelong custom he practiced until a few days before he died. In 1840, Draper began to supplement this written correspondence with interviews. To accomplish this, Draper traveled extensively through the Alleghenies and the South, finding old pioneers and recording their reminiscences. Explaining his inspiration to go to these great lengths, Draper once wrote to a friend: "I am very passionately devoted to the Pioneer history of the romantic West—I keep delving away at it, more for the real love I have for the thing itself than anything else."[12] Throughout his early adulthood, Draper would try his hand at several careers, such as clerking and farming, even testing the waters of the newspaper business for a short time in Mississippi. He studied at two different colleges, but history and collecting were his first loves, and to them he would return whenever possible.

In February 1848, Draper's college friend, Charles Larrabee, was a delegate to Wisconsin's constitutional convention. Later that year, Larrabee attempted to lure Draper to Wisconsin. Larrabee had influential friends in Wisconsin, among them Governor Dewey; he was confident he could help Draper land the directorship of the state library in Madison. Failing that, there was the possibility of "an easy and honorable post" with the new state university, or finally the librarianship of the historical society.[13] Beset by family obligations and personal equivocation, Draper declined. But Larrabee did not let up, sending Draper repeated offers of employment, as well as promotional literature singing the praises of Madison.

Finally, in 1852, the time was right. Some of Draper's filial commitments lessened when his uncle Peter Remsen died. Draper was also seeking employment that would, in his own words, "leave me a goodly portion of time in which to prosecute my labors in the field of western history."[14] Larrabee's proposals now seemed more attractive. But when Draper finally arrived in Madison in October of that year, his job prospects had dried up. Larrabee was no longer in a position to help him find other opportunities, and winter was about to set in.

Despite these unfavorable prospects, Draper stayed in Madison. He was supported by a modest inheritance from his uncle, and he found a friendly reception among his fellow Baptists. Thanks to his inheritance, Draper needed only part-time employment to supplement his income, leaving him free to work on his biography of a backwoods surveyor and adventurer named Daniel

Boone.[15] With an eye trained on employment, Draper introduced himself to influential members of the Wisconsin Historical Society, whom he impressed with his erudition and ideas for expanding the Society's activities.

Draper later reflected that the Society in 1852 was going through stages similar to those experienced by "kindred institutions—an early organization by the foresight of a hopeful few, followed by neglect, a brief sickly existence, and an early death . . . resuscitated again and again."[16] Not surprisingly for a western historian, Draper likened the Society to "the old Kentucky hunter, his trusty gun . . . once accidentally failing him, he would 'pick the flint, and try the old rifle again.'"[17]

Foremost among the Society's problems was a split among members over what type of organization it should be. On one side was Charles Lord, a Massachusetts native who favored a restricted membership conferring social status and denoting "cultural attainment."[18] On the other side stood Lyman Draper, who envisioned a more democratic society with an open, dues-paying membership. In the midst of the debate, Draper would write that he was "exceedingly anxious . . . to have our Society flourish equal to any other in the Union."[19]

As it turned out, Draper was just the man to "pick the flint, and try the old rifle again." In January 1853, having endeared himself to several prominent Society members including Governor Leonard Farwell, then president of the Society, Draper was admitted as a member and named to the Society's executive committee. That winter, Draper sat down with his old friend Charles Larrabee to write a charter for the Society. "The object of the Society" the men wrote, "shall be to collect, embody, arrange, and preserve in authentic form a library of books, pamphlets, maps, charts, manuscripts, papers, paintings, statuary, and other materials illustrative of the History of the State."[20] They went on to establish that the Society should "exhibit faithfully the antiquities of the past and present condition and resources of Wisconsin. It should promote the study of history by lectures, and diffuse and publish information relating to the description and history of the state."[21] Draper's hand was clearly evident within its mandate: "to secure from oblivion the memory of its early pioneers and to obtain and preserve narratives of their exploits, perils and hardy adventures . . ."[22]

The charter was promptly accepted by the Society's executive committee, and it passed through the legislature without a hitch. Under its charter, the Society was recognized as a corporate body endowed with the authority to collect broadly, have an open membership, and receive funding from the state.

Additionally, to strengthen the bond between the Society and the State government, Draper and Larrabee renamed the organization from "The Historical Society of Wisconsin," which was the name used in the Society's 1849 constitution, to "The State Historical Society of Wisconsin."

In January 1854, the Society adopted a robust new constitution that, among other things, confirmed the new name; created four levels of membership and the amount of dues required of each; and established various offices in the Society and their respective duties. In accordance with Draper's wishes, the new constitution also defined a host of duties for a strengthened Executive Committee. Previously, this three-member committee was directed only to "have charge of the affairs of the Society," to report on the committee's activities, and to report on the condition of the Society.

Under the new constitution, the Executive Committee was directed to meet at least monthly to "supervise and direct all the financial and business concerns of the Society." Additionally, the committee could purchase items for the library, schedule lectures, fill most vacancies in the Society, arrange an annual address before the Society of an orator of their choosing, publish "written matters of the Society", and make an annual report to the Society, accompanied by any suggestions the committee may have. In later years, the size of the Executive Committee would grow, and the committee would be renamed the Board of Curators, which today still governs the Society's operations.

What began as a club of history-minded amateurs seven years earlier was about to embark on a remarkable period of growth and innovation. For the next three decades, the Society would be guided by Draper's forward-looking, democratic vision and matchless leadership.

Draper Takes the Reins

Lyman Draper was elected to the post of corresponding secretary of the Society in January 1854. He set out at once to increase the size and scope of the Society's research collections. Though he had little money, Draper was not without currency. He cajoled dozens of prominent historians and public figures, naming them honorary members of the Society while soliciting copies of their works. Books began trickling in, a couple dozen at a time at first.[23] Draper also convinced the legislature to print extra copies of government publications so he could exchange volumes with other institutions. In his first year at the helm, the Library grew to more than two thousand books and pamphlets, necessitating a move from the capitol to the basement of Madison's First Baptist Church. There the Society Library would remain for the next ten years, growing steadily. Eventually outgrowing even these quarters, it would move again into rooms of the new state capitol just after the Civil War.[24]

Draper was not shy about asking for donations for the Society. In his first annual report to the Society in 1854, he submitted a list of "Objects of Collection Desired by the Society" which included: "Manuscript statements and narratives of pioneer settlers—old letters and journals relative to the early history and settlement of Wisconsin, and of the Black Hawk War; biographical notices of our pioneers, and of eminent citizens, deceased; and facts illustrative of our Indian tribes, their history, characteristics, sketches of their prominent chiefs, orators and warriors."[25] Draper also requested newspapers, books, pamphlets, "drawings and descriptions" of Indian mounds, "curiosities" that happened to have been found in Wisconsin, convention minutes, and a host of other items. Draper knew several bookstore owners and publishers on the East Coast with whom items could be deposited, and who would forward the items to the growing collection in Madison. In exchange, Draper placed the donors on a list and promised them "equivalent publications of the Society."[26]

Propelling Draper to this obsession for collecting was his view that history was a literary activity that should focus on elegantly written, factually accurate depictions of the heroic deeds of the

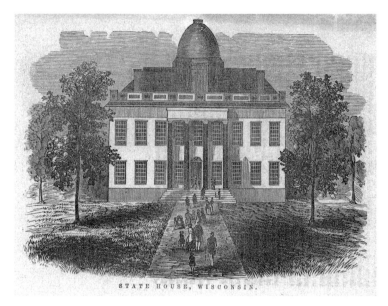

STATE HOUSE, WISCONSIN.

The Society's first home was in the Wisconsin Territorial Capitol,
pictured here as the building looked in 1859.

people who called Wisconsin home. While dreaming of the tomes
he would craft about the pioneers, Draper desired to get as close as
possible to the actual events, to record in minute and precise detail
the lives he wished to celebrate. Accordingly, Draper searched far
and wide for pioneers and their children, to gather their stories,
diaries, records, and reminiscences. Draper's definition of hero
was broad, seeing greatness in the men and women who settled the
frontier, the wives and farmers, the shopkeepers and the militia-
men and the Native Americans who had built their lives under
difficult circumstances.

Additionally, Draper understood that history was continually
being made. For example, at the beginning of the Civil War, he sent
a letter to several officers from Wisconsin's gathering regiments,
asking that they send him relics and curiosities. He encouraged
soldiers to keep diaries for a large Civil War collection he planned
to assemble, with which he planned to write an illustrated history
of Wisconsin's involvement in the war.[27] Like his other writing projects, this never came to fruition.[28]

Commemorative roster of Company G of the Twelfth Regiment,
Wisconsin Volunteer Infantry, created October 1861

Though Draper's own literary ambitions failed to bear fruit, one of his earliest successes at the Society was to publish, in 1855, the *First Annual Report and Collections of the State Historical Society of Wisconsin for the Year 1854*. Known colloquially as the *Wisconsin Historical Collections*, or simply the *Collections*, this 147-page document contained the obligatory reports from the executive committee and treasurer of the Society. Most significantly, however, the book included a dozen articles and original documents telling of early days in Wisconsin, with topics ranging from the French and Indian War to recollections from Green Bay in 1816–1817. Scattered throughout the volume were Draper's annotations, revealing the expertise he had acquired in Wisconsin history after only a few years in the state. With this volume, the Wisconsin Historical Society Press was born, a venture that continues to this day.

Printing these original documents served several purposes for Draper and the Society. Publishing documents was a means for Draper to preserve the material he collected, which was no small concern in the 1850s for an institution housed in the basement of a wooden building lit by candles and lamps. The *Collections* also made the raw material of history widely available, even to those who would never set foot in Madison. Draper realized these volumes could become useful in building the Library and the Society's manuscript collections. The books were excellent fodder for barter—for the rest of his tenure at the Society, Draper would trade volumes of the *Collections* for a host of books for the Library. And the names of people and institutions that donated to the Society were printed in subsequent volumes of *Collections*, which helped sow the seeds for future donations. Even better, Draper convinced members of the legislature to designate the *Collections* a departmental report, meaning that the state funded the printing costs for the eight thousand copies.

Every three years Draper assembled, annotated, and ushered into print a new volume of the *Collections*. These contained an increasing number of memoirs, journals, narratives, interviews, and other eyewitness accounts of Wisconsin's past. By the time the Society discontinued the series in 1915, the *Collections* numbered eleven thousand pages in twenty volumes, with more than one thousand documents. Among the treasures in the Collections are more than one hundred pioneer reminiscences from fur traders, farmwomen, and Indian elders, as well as diaries from travelers, soldiers, immigrants, and missionaries written while significant events in Wisconsin's development were unfolding, making the *Collections* the single most comprehensive record of life in Wisconsin during the colonial era.

With his ever-expanding collection, Draper needed help managing the growing Library. In 1856, he hired Madison book dealer Daniel S. Durrie to be the Society's librarian.[29] A New York native like Draper, Durrie was reserved and methodical, a stickler for detail, and the perfect complement to the utopian and idealistic Draper.[30] While Draper courted donors and politicians to his cause, Durrie handled the practical task of managing the growing collection. Durrie's historical tastes were democratic like Draper's, though Durrie had a strong interest in genealogy and local history.[31] For the next three decades, the two men worked together to build the Library and augment the Society's reputation among scholars across the country.

Librarian Daniel S. Durrie, seated in the two-story gallery occupied by the Society in the old South Wing of the state capitol from 1866 until 1883

Ten years after Durrie's arrival, the Society once again ran out of space. In January 1866, the legislature gave the Society three rooms in the new state capitol. There, the Society dwelt for the remainder of the nineteenth century, bringing in up to fifteen thousand visitors each year who saw firsthand the remarkable progress the Society had made in just over a decade. The Library had grown to twenty thousand volumes, the walls were adorned with selections from a growing portrait and painting collection, and visitors could peruse the Cabinet—the forerunner to the Society's museum—which, while lacking clear definition and purpose, contained interesting, odd, and otherwise noteworthy objects, including a silken tassel from the bed of Mary, Queen of Scots, a fragment of the famous warship *Constitution*, and a rosary of olive wood from the Mount of Olives.[32] On display were the principles of broad and impartial collecting that have guided the Society ever since. Library patrons could find not only standard newspapers

Stacks of the Society Library in 1898, when the Society occupied rooms in the third capitol building. At one time, gas light fixtures were used in this space, allowing an open flame to burn perilously close to flammable items such as the newspaper collection.

This small bookcase once housed the entire State Historical Library.

like the *Wisconsin State Journal*, but also the *Cherokee Pioneer*, the *African Repository*, and hundreds of colonial newspapers.

Draper simultaneously collected for the Society and for his own personal manuscript library, which was bequeathed to the Society upon his death in 1891. This collection, known colloquially as the Draper Manuscripts, consisted of original documents, Draper's transcriptions of documents, interview notes, Draper's correspondence, extracts from newspapers and other published sources, muster rolls, military records, and more, covering primarily the period between the French and Indian War and the

War of 1812 (ca. 1755–1815). Society staff organized the mass of partially sorted papers into 491 volumes divided into 50 series of varying lengths, arranged by geographic area, subject, and individual. Contained in the Draper Manuscripts are the personal papers of some legendary figures in early American history, including Daniel Boone, Mohawk chief Joseph Brant, George Rogers Clark, Simon Kenton, and Elizabeth Zane, among many others. The Draper Manuscripts soon became the Society's most famous and extensively used collection. In 1940, the Society began putting the collection on microfilm to make it more widely available and even published a nearly five-hundred-page guide for the collection.

The 1870s saw even more growth for the Society. In 1875, the Cabinet gained prominence when the Society acquired the Perkins Collection, a nine-thousand-item assortment of Native American stone and copper implements.[33] Yearly attendance grew, with the number of estimated visitors between 20,000 and 35,000.[34] By 1876, as the nation celebrated its first century, the Society had the largest library west of the nation's capital. And in a move that would have an impact on the Society in the coming decade, in 1876 the *Wisconsin State Journal* hired as its managing editor a twenty-three year old Massachusetts native named Reuben Gold Thwaites.[35]

Thwaites was born in Dorchester, Massachusetts, on May 15, 1853, the son of English immigrants. He spent his first thirteen years in Dorchester, before his family moved to Oshkosh, Wisconsin, in 1866. Thwaites spent the next six years working on the family farm while simultaneously working his way through studies normally reserved for college

Reuben Gold Thwaites, 1899. Thwaites assumed leadership of the Society in 1887, following the legendary Lyman Draper. During his twenty-six-year tenure, Thwaites created his own legend, increasing the Society's scope, modernizing its operations, and forging close ties with the University of Wisconsin.

students. In the early 1870s, Thwaites reported for the Oshkosh *Times*, then spent a year at Yale taking graduate-level courses. When he returned to Wisconsin in 1876 and began working at the *Wisconsin State Journal*, the job often brought him to the Society's rooms in the capitol building, where he soon became familiar with Lyman Draper.

By this time Draper had been casting an eye on potential successors. Draper was no longer a young man; drawing a lesson from "the ripening fruits of Summer and Autumn," Draper wrote, "we should, especially as we near the close of life, seek opportunities to provide for the enlightenment and happiness of mankind." For Draper this meant two things: finding the right man to care for the Society that he loved and labored to build, and finally writing the great biographies that would rescue western heroes from oblivion. In December 1884, Draper offered the young Thwaites a job as the Society's assistant corresponding secretary.[36] A month later, the Society elected Thwaites to the post.

Chapter Two

THE GOLDEN AGE

1880–1910s

For the next two years, Draper initiated his young protégé "into the mysteries of the Society," so that by the time Draper retired in 1887, Thwaites had already assumed management of the organization.[1] Thwaites bore some similarities to his predecessor—he was a newspaperman with an interest in history and, like Draper, a diminutive man, standing only four feet, seven inches tall. But Thwaites differed in significant ways. He was organized, methodical, and meticulous.

Thwaites made Wisconsin collecting a priority. He identified areas in which Society collections were lacking, raised funds to purchase items, and traveled across the state to obtain manuscripts that would fill the gaps. He detailed all he accomplished after one trip through the Fox Valley, noting the acquisition of "old letterbooks, diaries, memoranda and letters, fully 2,000 documents in all, illustrative of olden times, particularly the fur trade and the conduct of Indian affairs."[2]

Thwaites acquired the papers of notable Wisconsinites while also conducting interviews to create oral histories. He instituted the practice of sending Society staff to libraries

Reuben Gold Thwaites in his office

in other states, and later to Canada, England, and France, for the
purpose of copying documents relating to Wisconsin. Thwaites
also gathered records of contemporary society, especially those
sources describing the history of local matters, believing these to
be important not only as historical records but because they satis-
fied a genuine public interest.

While Draper and his librarian Daniel Durrie had developed their own idiosyncratic method for shelving and cataloging
materials, Thwaites cast about for the newest methods. Under
Thwaites, the Society adopted new practices in acquisitions, cataloging, research, and conservation of printed material. Thwaites
spent one summer in Europe visiting libraries, art galleries, and
museums to study how they worked. "If we are to keep step with
the times," Thwaites instructed, "it behooves us to bring to bear
upon the management of our institution the knowledge of what
is best elsewhere."[3]

One of the more significant differences between Draper and
Thwaites was the attitude each man took toward the Society's
relationship to the state. Though Draper had tied the Society's
financial footing to the state with the 1853 charter, he soured on
the arrangement after repeated, unsuccessful attempts to secure
funding for a fireproof building. Instead, Draper sought bequests
and donations from private donors. Draper did all of this with a
mind toward a self-sustaining institution, "no longer dependent
upon, or hampered by, any alliance with the State."[4] Only two years
after the state had generously provided expanded quarters for the
Society in the south wing of the capitol, Draper complained that:
"Ours can never be the useful, vigorous institution it should be,
until it attains its complete independence" [emphasis in original].[5]

Thwaites, on the other hand, understood that state support
allowed the Society to adopt methods very different from "its older
and more conservative sisters in the Eastern States."[6] Specifically,
state support encouraged the Society to be a popular organization
with an open membership, continually proving its worth "to the
public whose support it seeks," and seeking support for its work
from the "best public opinion of the Commonwealth."[7] Additionally, Thwaites noted that because the Society was entrusted with

public funds and property, it was necessarily staffed by "earnest, practical, experienced men, in whom both scholars and men of affairs may repose confidence."[8] Seeking state support for an institution in which these ideals were not realized was, in Thwaites's estimation, "hopeless."[9]

In practice, the Society formed a stronger bond with the state by developing a deeper connection with the University of Wisconsin, in Madison. Thwaites realized that most of the users of the Society's collections were college students. Accordingly, he chose to "hitch the Society's star" to the future of the university. Students were coming to Madison in greater numbers as enrollment increased fivefold in the last decade and a half of the nineteenth century. And university faculty encouraged students to use the Society's wide array of primary documents that were generally not available at the university library. Thwaites offered students unlimited access to the Society's stacks and opened additional rooms for study, an "unheard of liberality among non-university libraries at the time," recalled eminent historian Frederick Jackson Turner.

Frederick Jackson Turner's history seminar at work in an alcove at the Society in 1893, when the Society was still housed in the third capitol building

Turner, who regularly led his "little band of investigators" to the Society, later wrote that this greater freedom for their work "was the opening of a new life."[10]

Thwaites also understood the importance of the Cabinet, which he now referred to as the Museum. He began devoting resources to display the Society's portrait collection and artifacts more effectively. The Museum rooms were "thoroughly renovated, painted, and calcimined," Thwaites reported in 1892.[11] New display cases were built at the state carpenter shop to better exhibit "specimens and curios," while Thwaites introduced new methods of exhibiting pictures. All of this was done with the governor's recognition that exhibition halls entertaining more than thirty-five thousand visitors each year "should be placed in a condition fit to receive them."[12] While the Society had a reputation among scholars for the Library, the Museum, possessing much more interest for the general public, was a useful tool for public education through which the Society could "do excellent missionary work among the masses," Thwaites wrote.[13]

Running a library now packed with students and managing a museum that drew tens of thousands of visitors each year required more manpower—or, as it turned out, woman-power. In the late 1880s, Thwaites hired Annie Nunns, who eventually worked her way up to become the Society's assistant superintendent. Nunns, who would work for the Society until her death in 1942, was the first of many notable female hires Thwaites made in an effort to staff the Society with ambitious and intelligent young talent. These women were recent college graduates, devoted to their profession, whom Thwaites held to extremely high standards. In addition to Nunns, Mary Stuart Foster (known as "Mary, Queen of Stacks") and Iva Welsh were two other long-term Society employees. Nunns, Welsh, and Foster, who referred to themselves appropriately as "the Big Three," influenced and guided the Society from the turn of the century until the early years of World War II in a period known as "the Matriarchy."[14]

Having capable and spirited staff gave Thwaites the freedom to expand on the mission of the Society. In his travels about the state, Thwaites concluded that just as the Progressive Era university

Annie Nunns (left) was one of the Library matriarchs who guided the Society through the difficult years from World War I through the Great Depression. Society librarian Emma Hawley (right) was one of the professional young women hired by Reuben Gold Thwaites, shown here working on a typewriter she modified to accommodate library catalog cards. This 1892 photo was taken by Thwaites, who was also an amateur photographer.

considered its boundaries to be the borders of the state, so too should the Society be active throughout Wisconsin. Preserving and sharing history were duties rightly belonging to all interested people, and Thwaites sought to use the Society's influence and expertise to help.

In 1898, Thwaites successfully advocated for legislation that helped create a network of affiliated local historical societies. This legislation authorized the Society to provide uniform bylaws and require local societies to provide an annual report to the Society. Thwaites urged local groups and libraries to collect materials— diaries, letters, journals, books, and the like—relating to the history of their area. He wrote books and pamphlets, and lent advice whenever he was in the position to do so. He also spoke at gatherings, encouraging local leadership to build research centers, place historical markers, and develop museums, and he encouraged cooperation between local societies and schools to develop an interest in history among teachers and students. In 1899, Green Bay and Ripon became the first two local historical societies to affiliate with the Wisconsin Historical Society. One hundred years later, the

Society would have a network of almost four hundred affiliates, located in every corner of the state.

As the nineteenth century drew to a close, the Society enjoyed a reputation as one of the leading historical societies in the United States. In 1893, future president Theodore Roosevelt praised the Society as "the father of all such societies in the West."[15] Roosevelt continued, "Every American scholar, and in particular every American historian, is under a debt to your Society, and a debt to the State of Wisconsin, for having kept it up."[16]

The next year another future president, Professor Woodrow Wilson of Princeton College, commented on legislative support for the Society Library, writing, "I have no hesitation in saying that its loss or impairment would be nothing less than a national calamity, so far as the scholarship of the country is concerned. . . . Certainly no legislative grant could more directly contribute to the best interests of scholarship and patriotism than a grant to preserve such records as you possess."[17]

"Nearly Perfect" New Home

Even as those words were written, Thwaites stood on the cusp of possibly his most visible and enduring legacy: the construction of a separate building to house the Society. In one of his first annual reports, Thwaites wrote that the Society's quarters in the capitol building were woefully inadequate. The capitol, Thwaites wrote, was "a mere fire-trap," a sadly prophetic commentary, as the capitol would burn down in 1904. Neither was the capitol structurally sound. Thwaites wrote that "the state authorities are continually warning us that we are overloading the building, and look with well-grounded alarm upon the tons of matter which we annually add to our collections."[18] Yet to stop collecting was impossible. It was "no more practical to curb our progress, under natural conditions, than that of the age in which we live," Thwaites wrote.[19] The state government was growing as well, and Thwaites foresaw a time in the not-distant future when the Society's space would be coveted by the expanding government.

Being politically adroit, Thwaites was able to secure funding from the legislature in the mid-1890s, as well as cooperation from a variety of interested parties who wanted to use the new building. The result was a new, free-standing building, an impressive neo-classical structure that was both homage to the ancients and an exhibition of modern conveniences.

The new building, across the street from Bascom Hill on the university campus, took four years to construct. Adorned with columns without and within, its hallways were layered in marble wainscoting, with mosaic floors bearing the marks of various printers of antiquity, William Caxton and Aldus Manutius among others. The offices and public areas were furnished with stately mahogany and oak furniture.

The building was also equipped with the most modern technologies of the time. Door panels of beveled glass held in solid brass frames were set into the walls outside the double doors leading to the Library reading room, allowing visitors a glimpse of the electric circuitry that meandered through the walls of the building. These wires powered electricity throughout the building: motors in the janitors' repair shop, a telephone bank and electric bells on the

The construction of the new Society headquarters
in 1898, as seen from Bascom Hill

American Library Association group portrait, 1901, taken outside the Society headquarters building. The organization met in Madison because Thwaites wanted to draw attention to the Society's new building.

second floor used for communication with all parts of the building, electric elevators for visitors, and a "book-lift" for librarians.

A massive card catalogue in the reading room displayed modernity of a different kind: the implementation of new cataloging methods that helped researchers find what they were looking for. Thwaites wrote of the building admiringly, saying: "The building is as nearly perfect from a librarian's point of view, as possible under the circumstances."[20]

The first floor held public documents from all over Wisconsin, other parts of the country, and even some foreign governments. An adjoining room held manuscripts, newspapers, and photographs. Two marble stairways led to the upper floors, which housed administrative offices, university library offices, the Library reading room, and the Library stacks. At first, both the Society and the university libraries shared a single six-story wing on the south of the building. A decade later a north wing was built, which the university library then occupied.

The Library reading room on the second floor was the jewel of the new building. It had thirty-foot ceilings, columns lining the walls, and a bank of windows two stories high that flooded the

The elevator in the Society's headquarters, photographed shortly
after the completion of the new building in 1900

room with light. Its ceiling boasted ornate stained-glass skylights
that were set into the floor of the museum above. The reading
room was large enough to accommodate 240 people, while shelving along the walls housed 5,000 reference books "covering all
the principle branches of knowledge," available to all readers.[21]
For the next half century, the Society Library would serve as the
university's principal research collection.

The Reading Room in the Society's headquarters, ca. 1914

The third floor was home to a lecture hall, a variety of university classrooms, and administrative offices, but its most striking feature was the Visitor's Balcony. From this perch, visitors could look down upon the reading room. Adjoining the balcony were bookcases holding the Society's genealogical collections and materials of the art departments of both the Society and the university. Two special study rooms on this floor were reserved for students "engaged in protracted literary work."[22]

The fourth floor of the new building would "chiefly interest the general public," according to Thwaites, as it became the home of the Museum.[23] Here the Museum enjoyed more space, with handsome glass cases displaying notable objects from the Cabinet. Separate rooms were devoted to American ethnology, curiosities, Wisconsin war history, dishes and coins, and black-and-white art.[24] Portraits hung throughout the north gallery, while most of the museum space was lighted by skylights and windows. Both staircases led to the Museum, as did the passenger elevator, making the room accessible to the public. But the fourth-floor location was not ideal—it was unbearably hot in the summer, and the only staff devoted to the Museum was a janitor who had been assigned to the Society in its old quarters at the state capitol. But the Museum was gaining an expanded role in a Society increasingly dedicated to sharing the state's history more widely, with more people, and with the help of more groups outside of the Society's walls.

On August 20, 1900, the first cartload of books left the capitol and was drawn by horse to the new Society Library. Six weeks and a day later, with the help of several students, Society staff had moved all two hundred thousand books without losing a volume.[25] In fact, the only items lost during the move were the Society's correspondence files covering the years 1887 to 1900 and a desiccated black cat that had been sent to the Society some years before by a citizen of Darlington.[26] While the correspondence files were never seen again, it was later revealed that the black cat had actually been "borrowed" by two members of the Milwaukee Press Club in 1897 for a Milwaukee cat show. The mummified beast, which was never returned, was christened Anubis the Cat and has served as the mascot

Journalist Ellen MacQuarrie and an unidentified man look at Anubis the Cat, the mascot of the Milwaukee Press Club. The fossilized cat was stolen from the Society in 1897, though it was not discovered missing until the Society moved three years later.

of the Milwaukee Press Club for many decades. Anubis can still be seen on display at the Newsroom Pub in downtown Milwaukee.[27]

On February 27, 1904, not four years after the move, the state capitol building that once housed the Society burned to the ground, confirming Thwaites's assessment of the building as a "fire-trap." After the fire, the American Historical Association's Public Archives Commission, of which Thwaites was a member, surveyed Wisconsin's government records. The commission's report stated that, although damage to government documents had been limited by the fireproof vaults in which they'd been stored, the fire necessitated emergency storage that exposed these materials to a variety of hazards. Rather than create a new department of archives or wait to construct a new fireproof building for storage, the report's author suggested that noncurrent records be given to the Wisconsin Historical Society, "which has so amply shown its ability to care for them."

The Society had expended a great deal of effort to collect personal manuscripts, diaries, letters and the like, but little had been done in Wisconsin to preserve government documents. The Wisconsin Archives Act, which was passed by the legislature in 1907, paved the way for the Society to house, administer, and make these documents available. As then-current trends in historical scholarship stressed consulting original documents for authenticity, this new mission increased the Society's prestige among historians. Through numerous changes to the law, the Society today maintains the responsibility to collect, maintain, and make available for use the permanently valuable records of the state more than one hundred years later.

An Expanded Influence

The same year the Society began to administer the State Archives, an increase in the Society's appropriation enabled Thwaites to lure Charles E. Brown away from the Milwaukee Public Museum to head a newly created Museum Department.[28] Museum acquisitions were given a boost that year as the Society's executive committee

Museum curator Charles E. Brown

allotted four hundred dollars annually from the Antiquarian Fund, which had been established fifteen years earlier and was fed by membership dues and sales of duplicate volumes in the Library. This dual infusion of funds and expertise quickly produced noticeable results.

Brown immediately brought direction and order to the Museum. Under his guidance the collections were classified and rearranged, an accessioning system was installed, field collecting began in earnest, and special exhibits became a regular occurrence. Brown prescribed constraints on what would be collected, generally limiting items to the broad fields of history, ethnology, archaeology, and art. Though these were not strictly enforced, they helped to bring focus to the Museum collections. Meanwhile, Brown overhauled the displays in each of the rooms of the Museum to make them more attractive, which helped draw more visitors. Displays in turn influenced collecting as Brown identified and obtained items needed for new exhibits. He made a special effort to secure materials on Wisconsin's ethnic groups, religions, and obsolete farm implements, as well as items pertaining to the post office, lumbering, and firefighting.[29] Photographic collections also increased rapidly as a flood of donations came in, including a complete set of photographs of Union generals, 465 photographs of Confederate officers, and numerous photographs of American Indians.[30]

Nor did the Society's publications escape the notice of the tireless Thwaites. In fact, Thwaites had a reputation among scholars of the day as a first-rate editor, thanks to works like the monumental *Jesuit Relations* and the *Journals of Lewis and Clark*. The literarily prolific Thwaites edited 170 volumes and wrote 15 others, most for publishers other than the Society.[31] Early on in his tenure, Thwaites separated the *Wisconsin Historical Collections* from the *Proceedings*,

Ho-Chunk group in traditional dress, 1900. From the Charles Van Schaick collection. This is one of more than seventy-five thousand images available online at wisconsinhistory.org

reserving the *Collections* for primary historical material while the *Proceedings* constituted the records of Society activities. Frederick Jackson Turner called this "a significant step, emphasizing the distinction between source material and the secondary use of it, but recognizing both as legitimate activities of the Society."[32]

While Draper had established the Society Press in order to build the Library collections, Thwaites expanded the mission of the Press as he printed circulars and bulletins to assist local societies and history enthusiasts preserve and share history in their own backyards. The Society Press also issued a variety of catalogs and bibliographies to aid researchers using the Society Library and manuscript collections. Thus the Society, through its publications, was able to make its expertise widely available and, in the spirit of the Wisconsin Idea, expand its influence to every corner of the state. Additionally, the Society partnered with the university, the governor's office, and the Wisconsin Library Commission to form the Wisconsin History Commission, charged with observing, through a variety of publications, the semicentennial of the Civil War. Fittingly, Thwaites acted as the secretary and editor of this commission.

The Wisconsin History Commission reprinted several diaries and narratives written by Wisconsin soldiers during the war, including Julian Hinkley's *Narrative of Service with the Third Wisconsin Infantry* and Frank Haskell's account of the Battle of Gettysburg, which remains one of the most thorough and compelling accounts available detailing the deadliest battle ever fought in the Western Hemisphere. Original works, often by talented university students, have also stood the test of time. Ethel Hurn's *Wisconsin Women in the War* was a remarkable volume decades ahead of its time, focusing on women and the various, often surprising, roles they played during the Civil War. Frederick Merk, who would go on to study with Frederick Jackson Turner at Harvard and eventually succeed his mentor there, wrote for the commission *The Economic History of Wisconsin During the Civil War Decade*. A reviewer said of the book that it was clear the author had "done his work among the rich stores found in the library of the Wisconsin state historical society," and that authors of succeeding volumes in the series "will find it difficult to excel this work in the qualities that make the best type of historical writing."[33]

END OF AN ERA

On October 20, 1913, Thwaites made his final changes to the annual report that he planned submit to the Society at its annual meeting three days later.[34]

It was sixty-one years to the month since Lyman Draper had arrived in Madison. From humble beginnings, the Society had grown and flourished and was now in the midst of a golden age. A Library that once numbered fifty books and other items in a single bookcase had swelled to 364,649 volumes, overflowing its shelves and awaiting relief from chronic overcrowding by the construction, then underway, of a new stack wing. Legislative support for the Society had quadrupled since Thwaites accepted the directorship; private endowments had more than doubled; the Museum had become a force for popular education as Thwaites, in his report, looked to the future when the top floor of the new north wing would be dedicated to give the Museum even more gallery space; and staff had increased from four people to thirty-one.

Thwaites's annual report contained almost forty pages of accomplishments of the previous year, as well as aspirations for the year to come. He mentioned notable manuscript accessions, too numerous to itemize, flowing into the building, while staffing was now available to allow researchers to access the Society's ever-increasing trove of state documents from 7:45 a.m. to 10:00 p.m.[35] The Society received subscriptions for more than four hundred newspapers, of which more than three hundred originated in Wisconsin. Many of these were bound, not only for preservation, but to make them fit on shelves more efficiently, thus freeing room for even more material. Meanwhile, a team of catalogers classified accessioned material, while a research division responded to numerous requests for information, mostly from local history enthusiasts.

While new materials were being acquired by the Museum, older collections were being cataloged, and new displays were in development for the fourth-floor galleries. Many grammar and high schools, as well as university classes, traveled to the Society to view Museum displays, while Museum staff undertook "pilgrimages" to the shores of Lakes Mendota and Monona, leading students to sites of archaeological and historical interest. With the Society experiencing such "lusty growth," Thwaites predicted that "within five years it will be necessary to commence agitation for the construction of [a new] stack wing abutting on Park Street, which was contemplated in the original plans."[36]

After completing his annual report, Thwaites straightened up his office and went home. Later that evening suffering what felt like a kidney ailment, he went to the hospital.[37] On October 22, Thwaites died of apparent heart failure, sixty-eight years to the day since Chauncey Britt had printed his article asking for help from his brethren of the press to form a historical society.

Thwaites had seemed in robust health, and his sudden passing came as a shock to the Society. For twenty-six years, Thwaites had not only filled the considerable shoes of his legendary predecessor but in many ways had eclipsed Draper's achievements. Since taking over leadership of the Society in 1887, Thwaites had enlarged the Library rapidly, methodically collected Wisconsin manuscripts, and turned the publications program into an incredibly productive machine that had cranked out 183 volumes. Under Thwaites's leadership, the Society had evolved into a service institution, with a Library on the campus of the university from which it received most of its patrons and a Museum that was professionalized and employed in popular education, another of Thwaites's treasured goals. Under Thwaites, the Society met the needs of the scholar and academic, while not neglecting its popular appeal and usefulness for the amateur historian. The Society was no longer solely a Madison institution, having extended its expertise, services, and influence throughout the entire state.[38]

Unfortunately, one thing Thwaites did not do was prepare anyone to take his place. In the interim, his normal duties were farmed out to a variety of Society board members and staff. Within days of Thwaites's death, a search committee gathered to find a new superintendent—the term then used for the director. In another era, perhaps Annie Nunns, who was the de facto assistant superintendent of the Society, would have been named director. As it was, the committee did not consider Nunns or any of the qualified female staff then on board, choosing instead to court, fruitlessly, Frederick Jackson Turner, who had by then left Wisconsin for Harvard. The committee considered several other notable academics, archivists, and librarians, many of whom were greatly interested in the position.

In December 1913, the committee would alight on "a sound man of very great promise," Professor Milo Quaife of the Lewis Institute in Chicago, who had not even applied for the job.[39] While Quaife would share the youthfulness and vision of his predecessors, he was never able to assimilate with the Big Three, who remained devoted to Thwaites and never respected Quaife as his equal. This led to political and administrative difficulties, which abbreviated Quaife's tenure. This tension, along with the deprivations of a world war and the economic collapse a decade later, combined to draw the Society into several decades of decline.

Chapter Three

DOOMSDAY

1910s–1940s

Milo Milton Quaife was born on October 6, 1880, in Nashua, Iowa. At thirty-three, he was the youngest candidate considered by the Society's search committee. Quaife was well educated; he received his undergraduate degree from Grinnell College, a master's degree from the University of Missouri, and a doctorate from the University of Chicago. Quaife's considerable abilities as an editor and writer shone through in his long list of publications, which then included the four-volume *Diary of James K. Polk*, several articles, a thesis on the *Doctrine of Non-Intervention with Slavery in the Territories*, and a local history, *Chicago and the Northwest.*[1] Quaife was a first-rate scholar, though his abilities as an administrator were yet to be revealed.

Quaife chose to continue and improve on several of Thwaites's programs. He sent a staff member to Washington to search the files of various federal departments for documents relating to Wisconsin. In 1915, the program's first year, the Society's

Milo Quaife was just thirty-three years old when he was hired as Society director in January 1914. Under Quaife's leadership, the Society began publishing the *Wisconsin Magazine of History*, which continues to this day.

field representative sent back 10,000 Photostatic copies. Unfortunately the cost for this work was considerable, and the project had to be scaled back. Quaife also used the authority granted by the 1907 Wisconsin Archives Act to solicit records of the executive department and other agencies. Quaife's skill in acquiring new manuscripts won him the title of "the new Draper" by one friend of the Society.[2]

Quaife's most substantial changes were to the Society's publications. The Society continued to issue literature that had become, by this time, normative for the Society: bulletins of information, catalogs, and bibliographies. Quaife wanted to use the written word to improve communication between the Society and its membership, as well as the people of Wisconsin. He began publishing the monthly *Wisconsin History Bulletin*, which was sent to 325 newspapers and contained bits of local history, as well as mention of Society activities. Quaife also wrote a weekly syndicated history column for the United Press. By 1914, it was printed in forty-two Sunday papers across the country

Quaife introduced a new series titled *Wisconsin Historical Publications*. This was a continuation of the *Collections* under a different name. While Draper and Thwaites had used the *Wisconsin Historical Collections* to document the prehistory and settlement of Wisconsin, Quaife and his staff used the new series to document the political development of the state. Quaife eventually would publish several volumes documenting Wisconsin's achievement of statehood.

In September 1917, Society's editorial staff unveiled yet another new publication: a quarterly journal titled the *Wisconsin Magazine of History*, in which shorter, secondary studies would be printed. Quaife introduced the magazine to readers by noting that "the historical interests of the professional scholars among our membership are catered to by numerous historical reviews," hence the magazine was meant to appeal to intelligent laypeople "without sacrificing in any way the scholarly ideals of the society." Each issue included articles by scholars such as Dr. Louise Phelps Kellogg, Professor Carl Russell Fish, and Milo Quaife himself.

The *Wisconsin Magazine of History* connected the Society to Wisconsinites more closely than many of its other ventures. Every

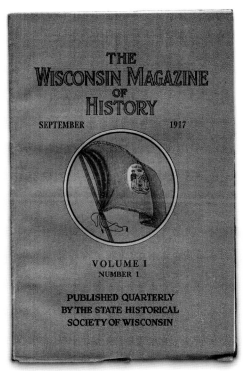

The first issue of the *Wisconsin Magazine of History*, published September 1917

three months a new issue of the magazine brought a little piece of the Society to homes and library shelves across the state. The magazine has been published every quarter without interruption since 1917, making it one of Quaife's most enduring legacies.

WORLD WAR I

From the beginning of his tenure, Quaife attempted to peacefully assimilate with long-time staffers, the Big Three especially. Quaife gave Annie Nunns the official title of assistant superintendent, which was in line with the actual duties she performed. Quaife also increased salaries and sought to give credit where it was due. Yet he never gained the trust or respect of the matriarchs, and their distrust eventually spread to the Board of Curators.

Compounding problems within the Society was the outbreak of World War I. War increased the Society's expenses in unforeseen ways. Federal regulation of newsprint production threatened the Society's ability to continue collecting newspapers. Restrictions on the supply of flour, which was used as an adhesive, impeded manuscript repairs. Restrictions on travel slowed visits by school groups to the Museum to a trickle, while the increase in the costs of books, heating, postage, and a litany of other expenses strained the Society's budget, which had already been shrinking in recent years.[3]

Yet the war's most distressing toll on the Society was felt by its employees. Within a fifteen-month period between 1917 and 1918, the twenty-eight-person Society staff shrank to eight as most of its employees went into military service or industries that supported the war effort.[4] "To him and all his kind we offer a reverent Godspeed," Quaife wrote in honor of a Library employee who resigned to join the war effort. "The nobility of their offering is inspiring enough; that it should have been necessary in the full light of the twentieth century is one of the ghastliest facts in human history."[5]

By this time, Quaife was already on the hot seat for mishandling a seemingly innocuous issue: the Society policy on lending certain reference materials via interlibrary loan. This escalated into a litany of charges of mismanagement of the Society, many of them exaggerated or simply false, made by a disgruntled patron from Menasha. Though an investigation largely vindicated Quaife, he lost the confidence of the Board of Curators. Through an arrangement of his own design, Quaife stepped down as superintendent to lead the Society's newly reorganized editorial division and publications program. Quaife lingered for three years after being demoted before eventually moving on to a long and fruitful career in Michigan as a writer and historian.

Discord and Decline

Succeeding Quaife was fifty-three-year-old Joseph Schafer, a Grant County native with degrees from the University of Wisconsin.[6]

Schafer was an impeccable scholar. But he had little administrative skill and no experience working with the press or legislature. As a result, he struggled unsuccessfully to place the Society back on a path toward innovation and broadly imagined service. Though the war had lasting, negative effects for the Society, a more talented director may have lessened the impact by cultivating political and popular support. Instead, Schafer committed himself to a major research project that the Society had no way of completing.

Schafer imagined a project similar to the Domesday (or "Doomsday") Book of William I, King of England. King William's Domesday Book was compiled in 1086 after an exhaustive survey of England to determine who held what property and wealth in the country. The aim of Schafer's Doomsday Project was to gather as much information as possible about Wisconsinites at the most local level imaginable in order to, in Schafer's words, "point out the influence upon Wisconsin history of even very local and seemingly humble individuals."[7] He envisioned a goldmine of data based on available plat maps, including historical data mined with the help of an army of researchers—teachers, students, and librarians— all working under the supervision of trained historians. The data would reveal the complex relationships between Wisconsinites and their environment, from pioneer days up to the twentieth century. Schafer thought this geosocial survey would take sixteen to twenty years to complete.

Had Schafer's Doomsday Project worked as he intended, it would have been a commendable example of cooperation between the Society and a multitude of local entities—schools, libraries, and local historical societies, among others. Schafer, however, was never able to stir the enthusiasm of his needed collaborators. When the Society finally did print the first installments of its Doomsday Book in September 1920, the volumes fell far short of expectations. The project was simply too ambitious even for a scholar of Schafer's caliber.

In the early 1920s, the Society's state appropriations began to decline. This led to discord, as private funding sources long reserved for the Museum's operating budget were diverted to pay for the Society's operating expenses. Nevertheless, Museum

director Charles E. Brown kept the Museum active and expanding on a shoestring budget. Brown extended the Museum's reach
beyond Madison as he prepared displays of artifacts, implements,
and photographs to circulate throughout the state. He traveled
across Wisconsin, talking to schools, advising local museums and
historical societies, and giving interviews to newspapers and radio
stations. In addition, Brown worked with several groups, including
the University of Wisconsin and the Madison Park and Pleasure
Drive Association, among others, to preserve Indian mounds in
various parts of Madison and southern Wisconsin.[8]

One-thousand-year-old American Indian burial mounds shaped like birds and
animals grace a hilltop in the Wisconsin River Valley in southwestern Wisconsin.

Portrait of Frances Fairchild (left), wife of Governor Lucius Fairchild, wearing a court gown designed by Charles Frederick Worth of Paris. Mrs. Fairchild wore this gown in 1880, at the Spanish court of King Alfonso XII and Queen Teresa in Madrid, Spain. Today Mrs. Fairchild's dress (right) is part of the Museum's collections.

The Museum's activities improved the Society's visibility among several audiences, including schoolchildren (Brown arranged a regular philatelic display to draw young stamp collectors), their parents and teachers, as well as the donors whose funding made the acquisitions and exhibits possible. Additional funding from the Wisconsin Legislature kept the Museum functioning well until the Great Depression, at which point public and private money dried up and put the Museum, like the Society's other programs, on hold. Yet throughout the 1920s it was the Museum, alone among the Society's divisions, that retained the dedication to public education and service that had been the hallmark of the Thwaites years.

Another bright spot for the Society during this time was Louise Phelps Kellogg. Kellogg was a longtime Society staffer who was hired by Thwaites as a research assistant in 1901, shortly after Kellogg received a PhD from the University of Wisconsin. Kellogg helped compile several volumes of the *Wisconsin Historical*

Louise Phelps Kellogg working at her desk

Collections and did substantial work indexing the series. Kellogg also edited five volumes of material from the Draper Manuscripts, three with Thwaites and two after his death. Kellogg had rightly earned the title senior research associate by answering legions of queries on just about every conceivable topic touching Wisconsin's past. Like Brown, Kellogg traveled throughout the state, speaking to societies and clubs. Ultimately Kellogg gained a national reputation as the leading scholar of French and British regimes in the Great Lakes area, and she would publish notable volumes on these topics in the 1920s and '30s.

On the balance, while the 1920s roared, the Society faltered. The Society's publications lacked the focus of the Thwaites years and suffered materially with the departure of Milo Quaife, who proved himself a first-rate editor and writer. The Library and Manuscript divisions shared the oddly juxtaposed problems of faltering accessions yet too little space.

Meanwhile, as the University of Wisconsin grew, Library resources were strained. Though the Society building was little more than two decades old, and the north wing had just been completed in 1915 to give the Society and the university each their own wing, the Library stacks were already filled to overflowing. Newspaper storage had to be created in a steam tunnel, while boxes and books cluttered the stack floors. Neglect of routine maintenance led to a leak in the roof that nearly damaged Museum

Robert La Follette Sr. and
Robert La Follette Jr.

items nearby. The Society and university staff searched for relief and considered separating the two libraries. The university nearly secured money for a Robert M. La Follette Memorial Library in the late 1920s, while the Society failed to secure an appropriation to build an annex that would house newspapers, periodicals, and the State Archives. Soon the Great Depression put all such ambitious programs on hold.

The Great Depression

It is difficult to assess the root of the Society's troubles during the Depression years. Even before the effects of the crash were felt in Wisconsin, the Society had for several years failed to connect as strongly with donors, legislators, and the people of Wisconsin as it had during the Thwaites years. Yet the drop in income the Society felt as a result of the Depression was severe, which worsened the Society's decline throughout the 1930s. Income from private sources dropped eighteen percent during that decade, and by the end of the 1930s, state appropriations had fallen to their lowest levels since 1914.[9]

The Society's executive committee and Superintendent Schafer faced difficult choices as they struggled to maintain essential

services. The book fund was slashed, causing a steep decline in
accessions; manuscript collecting, bookbinding, and shelving also
suffered under tight budgets. The Museum appropriation was cut
by more than half, and as Museum director Brown turned his attention to a Works Progress Administration project, the Museum
stagnated for the next decade.[10] Not one staff member received a
raise from 1931 to 1937, while many upper-level employees took
pay cuts. Meanwhile, the Society and the university butted heads
several times during the decade over the operating and maintenance costs of the building they'd shared for three decades.

Society activities slowed to a crawl during the 1930s. To save
on ever-increasing publications costs, the Society's annual *Proceedings* were printed in the *Wisconsin Magazine of History*. In 1935, the
Society finally published Louise Phelps Kellogg's long-completed
volume *The British Regime in Wisconsin and the Northwest*, paying for
its publication by delaying Schafer's *The Winnebago-Horicon Basin*,
which would be the fourth, and ultimately last, installment of the
ill-conceived Doomsday Books. Private funding covered the cost
of reprinting a couple of arcane pharmacy texts. The occasional
efforts to print the Draper Manuscripts ended when the Society
began reproducing them on a new medium, microfilm, which
was a more cost-effective way to make the material available to
researchers outside of Madison. Meanwhile, as the 1930s came to a
close, Joseph Schafer began work on the last book he would usher
into print, the 925-page *Memoirs of Jeremiah Curtain*.

Road to Recovery

The early 1940s seemed an unlikely time for the Society's fortunes
to improve, as the world was engaged in another world war that the
United States would soon enter. In fact, the 1940s seemed to start
off quite poorly, as attrition took its toll on an aging Society staff.
The list of staffers who retired or passed away in the early 1940s is
a who's who of people who had run the Society for decades, many
of whom had been hired by Reuben Gold Thwaites. On January
27, 1941, Joseph Schafer died following a brief illness, after leading

the Society for twenty-one difficult years. For several months he was replaced on an interim basis by Annie Nunns, the Society's first female, albeit acting, director. Not one year later, Miss Nunns also died. Nunns had worked for the Society since 1889 and was one of the last living links to Lyman Draper.[11] Lillian Beecroft, whom Thwaites had hired in 1908, retired on July 1, 1941, while Louise Kellogg died the next year. Mary Stuart Foster, who had worked for the Society for forty-eight years, retired in 1944; Charles E. Brown, who ran the Museum for almost thirty-six years, and Iva Welsh, chief cataloger, each retired the same day as Foster.

Into this void stepped a new generation of talent that would place the Society on the road to recovery and reverse two challenging decades of decline. Meanwhile, the worldwide struggles against communism and fascism highlighted the need for Americans to better understand their past. And the Civil War Centennial in the early 1960s and the American Revolution Bicentennial in 1976 renewed Wisconsinites' interest in their own heritage. The Society would respond to these and other demands of the mid-twentieth century under its next two directors, Edward Alexander and Clifford Lord. Once again the Society would stand on the threshold of possibilities.

Chapter Four

LORD'S WAY

1940s–1950s

Before she died, Annie Nunns encouraged the Society to find someone cut from the same cloth as Reuben Gold Thwaites as a successor for Schafer.[1] After a long search that stretched into the summer of 1941, the Board of Curators chose Dr. Edward Alexander, who seemed to possess the better qualities of several former directors. Like Draper and Thwaites, Alexander was a young and energetic visionary; like Quaife and Schafer, he was a scholar, with a PhD from Columbia University and undergraduate and graduate degrees from the University of Iowa, in his home state.[2] Though only in his mid-thirties, Alexander had already directed the New York State Historical Association for more than seven years, where he edited a quarterly historical magazine; his "energy, tact, and ability made him the logical candidate," according to William A. Titus, then president of the Society.[3]

Alexander's short tenure paralleled the nation's involvement in World War II and restricted what he could accomplish. And yet, he and his team renewed the Society's ambitious vision that had gone dormant for the preceding two decades. Alexander had a special interest in local historical societies and expressed his hope that every county in Wisconsin might have one.[4] World War II strained local history efforts but also provided a clear purpose. As Alexander noted, "Institutions which do not immediately serve the war effort tend to decline rapidly, and nearly all educational projects have hard sledding."[5] Yet Alexander believed the study of local history "inculcates the highest kind of patriotism"; "America," he argued, "is big and impersonal and thus difficult to understand and appreciate as a whole."[6] In contrast, a local community is "warm and human and personal, especially when its personality has been made known."[7]

Even in wartime, Wisconsin's local historical societies successfully kept their members involved. Alexander did what he could to encourage the local societies, publishing accounts of their activities in the *Wisconsin Magazine of History* and working to codify stronger partnerships with the local organizers. Alexander hoped to circulate displays from the Society's Museum collections around the state to "help them become even more active educational forces." While renewing the Society's commitment to local history was important, Society staff also had to scrape the figurative rust off several programs that had languished for the better part of the 1920s and '30s. The Society Press needed direction to remain relevant in a changing publishing landscape, and the Society's oldest venture, the Library, was in desperate need of space for its ever-growing book and manuscript collections, as was the Museum.

Decades of poverty and neglect had left the Library in desperate straits. Both the Society Library and the university library were "disgracefully overcrowded" with too many books, not enough room for students, and overcrowded staff work rooms. A 1943 report concluded that the university needed its own library and a doubling of its book budget. To alleviate overcrowding, staffs of the Society and university libraries worked out coordinated collecting procedures to reduce duplication. Additionally, Alexander enthusiastically embraced microfilm. The Library bought its first newspapers on microfilm in 1942, and the next year Alexander employed staff to microfilm the Society's newspapers. Within a year the Library contained more than one thousand reels of microfilm. All hard-copy subscriptions to out-of-state newspapers ended in 1945 and were replaced with papers available on film, saving much-needed space.

The Society's Museum had also staggered through the Depression years, with outdated displays and inconvenient galleries on the fourth floor. But Alexander saw enormous latent potential: "The treasures of the Society's Library and Museum . . . were crying

Society historians Kenneth Duckett and Alan E. Kent use the microfilm reader
in the Society's former manuscript room.

out to be used." In the early 1940s, Alexander arranged new exhibits that kept modern concepts in mind, taking into account
"structure, space, form, color, and light as a unified whole." Alexander hired additional staff for the Museum and revised collection
policies. For the first time, exhibits were placed in prominent first-
floor galleries, which patrons passed on their way to the Library.
Believing that "museums need not look like morgues," Alexander installed lighted cases to improve viewing. Exhibits changed
frequently, covering a variety of themes including the circus and
turn-of-the-century "do-it-yourself" projects. Despite wartime travel
restrictions and tight resources, Museum attendance rose.

Underlying all of his efforts was Alexander's conviction that "a
historical society must have popular appeal if it is to have influence
in its particular community."[8]

The Plumber from Kenosha

The Society's rebirth began with Alexander and blossomed under his successor, Clifford Lord, who became Society director in 1946 when a dispute over salary led Alexander to resign. Another young and ambitious scholar, Lord brought big ideas and the conviction that things should happen quickly. There was little that Lord did not want the Society to tackle, and less that he thought could not be resolved before lunch if everyone just put their hearts and minds to the task. Lord's political and cultural education was molded by the Depression, the New Deal, and the worldwide battles against fascism and communism. Lord and his new assistants, mostly young World War II veterans, put their distinctive stamp on the century-old State Historical Society.

Lord and his staff believed they were not just running a historical agency; they were making history in their own time. They faced new opportunities and fresh problems, including the challenge of "relevance." What useful purpose did the historical society serve in the new atomic age? What endeavors would justify the expense of maintaining it? The answers lay in recasting the Society as an institution that would address modern problems. For Lord, the critical study of the realities of American life served as a tonic against the dangers of the totalitarian ideologies that Americans had fought against, both in the recently ended World War II and in the new cold war.

Lord viewed history as part of the great "battle for the minds and souls of men," a requirement for citizens to "know and understand" the basis of American democracy.[9] As he said in an address on the importance of state and local history: "The study of history . . . clearly demonstrates the power of the individual to make his contribution, to shape or help shape the course of events; to make history where history is made—at the local level."[10]

Lord and his staff knew they needed to reach popular audiences if they wanted to achieve this goal. Lord and his assistants went so far as to create a mythical staff member, "the plumber from Kenosha," who was "called into every policy conference, into the discussion of every new program, every promotional or publicity

Clifford Lord, shown here examining a book in the Society's manuscript collection, directed the Society from 1946 to 1958. An ambitious, energetic, and creative man, Lord was instrumental in reviving the Society after the strains of two world wars and the Great Depression.

release."[11] Lord noted this fictitious plumber was a helpful addition to the staff, if a slightly difficult person to reach. As Lord wrote, "We do wonder a bit . . . just how does one capture his imagination, his interest, his appreciation, his enthusiasm?"[12] The Society would still serve university scholars and professional academics, but a renewed Society needed to reach men and women of all backgrounds and professions to be fully relevant in the mid-twentieth century.

Encouraging the study of local history was a logical priority for a Society whose leadership desired a closer connection to the people of Wisconsin. In every community around Wisconsin there were, and are, people who are interested in the episodes, achievements, heartaches, and struggles that make up a community's history—stories about schools, churches, businesses, and families, as well as the events that have shaped the community's identity. Local historical societies abound in Wisconsin, groups that have been busily engaged in preserving objects and accounts of the lives that influenced their particular community.

A large measure of Lord's program to revitalize the Society after World War II focused on aiding local societies and local historians to better understand their communities. The study of local history, Lord wrote, "cannot help but make us better citizens," while it also had the power to "make us better people, for it cannot help but give us insight into how human beings act and react."[13] Most important, however, the study of local history would restore the centrality of the individual in a sometimes all-too-impersonal world. As Lord explained, "When you get back to the locality you see that history, with God's help, is made by men. We witness it every day. It is so obvious we overlook it."[14]

Lord also recognized the international importance of local history: "We are engaged today in the greatest battle for the minds and souls of men and women which the modern world has witnessed," he wrote in early 1950. "Study local history and we dissipate the fog of intangibles. . . . We come to appreciate the significance of the American experiment. We see the essential elements it has to offer to all men everywhere as a model and an inspiration. We begin to comprehend why democracy is still potentially the greatest revolutionary force on the face of the earth."[15]

Appropriately, then, Lord worked to improve the relationship between the Wisconsin Historical Society and the local historical societies that had become affiliated with it.

After World War II ended, the Society took an active role in helping local organizations place historical markers on historically significant sites. In 1944, Governor Walter Goodland, foreseeing the end of World War II and the increased tourist travel that would ensue in the state, appointed a committee to study how best to identify historic locations in Wisconsin. Just after the war, the state began marking historic locations such as the site of Jean Nicolet's landing near Green Bay. In 1950, the Wisconsin Historical Sites and Markers Committee created a standardized design for new markers, made of cast aluminum and painted brown with cream-colored lettering and a "ferocious-looking badger."[16] The next year, the first of these standard-ized markers was placed at the Peshtigo Fire Cemetery.

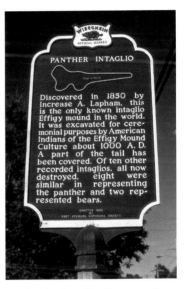

Panther intaglio effigy mound historical marker in Fort Atkinson

The markers program, which continues to this day, has been a tangible and enduring means for the Society and local communities to work together. While the Society approves new marker applications, individu-als and groups pay for the signs themselves and choose the subject matter. Markers must denote places of historical inter-est that are significant enough to warrant commemoration on a local, state, or national level. Markers also must touch on one of a wide array of categories, including archaeology, archi-tecture, culture, events, ethnic groups and associations, geology, legends, natural history, and, of course, people. Today more than 540 historical markers dot the state.

Society staff also renewed their efforts to modernize and ex-pand the Archives in the post–World War II era. Under Lord's direction, the Society began collecting historical records at the national level in broad topical areas. Lord acquired the records of the Cyrus Hall McCormick family and the McCormick Harvesting Machine Company (later known as International Harvester). Lord expanded the Society's efforts to collect union records when he acquired the records of the American Federation of Labor and other large industrial unions. Most significantly for the long term, Lord created a national collecting program in 1968, titled the Mass Communications History Center. This center developed media collections that included broadcasting, print journalism, and advertising. One advocate summed up the center's importance by writing, "Communication is the cement that will hold our society together—if, indeed, it can be held together." Within its first year, the Mass Communications History Center acquired one of its most significant collections, the papers of the National Broadcasting Company. This collection would grow to include papers filling more than 600 boxes and 3,000 recordings.

Just two years later, the University of Wisconsin formed the Wisconsin Center for Film and Theater Research. The Society has

McCormick poster, ca. 1882. The McCormick-International Harvester Company Collection contains documents, publications, photographs and films related to Cyrus Hall McCormick and the International Harvester Company. The collection, which doubled in size with new acquisitions in the 1990s, includes more than twelve million pages and items dating from 1753 to 1985. These items document the history of the agricultural equipment industry, the McCormick family, and topics as diverse as advertising, technology, labor, business, rural life, philanthropy, architecture, Virginia, Chicago, and many more.

partnered with this Center for more than fifty years. Originally intended to document theater history, the Wisconsin Center for Film and Theater Research began to include television and film in its collection early in its existence. This Center has gathered personal papers, films, photographs, and myriad other materials from some of the biggest names and organizations in Hollywood. Highlights include a massive collection of materials from United Artists and MTM Enterprises, which produced The Mary Tyler Moore Show, as well as notable individuals such as Kirk Douglas and Hal Holbrook. Today, the Society houses the Center's impressive archives, which have grown to include 20,000 motion pictures, television shows, and videotapes; 2 million still photographs and promotional graphics; several thousand sound recordings, and historical records and personal papers from some of the most notable figures in early Hollywood.

Another important step came in 1954 when Clifford Lord hired Paul Vanderbilt to curate the Society's visual materials collection. Vanderbilt held a deep and subtle appreciation for a photograph. He wrote that a "particular moment . . . instead of evaporating like other moments into the intangible vastness of time, is held fast as if that yesterday were also today and tomorrow."[17] Until his retirement in 1972, Vanderbilt exercised wide authority to organize, collect and interpret the Society's Iconographic Collections, as they came to be known.

A New Generation of Historians

Some of the most vigorous development in the Society's programs took place in Lord's outreach to schools and communities. Not since Thwaites's untimely death had a Society director done so much to reach out to schools and communities, making "history palpable and alive—not merely dates and places in a book."[18]

In 1947, the Society launched an ambitious program for young people, intending "to increase greatly the tangible service we render to the people of the State."[19] In the spring of that year, the Society established prototype "junior historian chapters" in six

middle and high schools.[20] Student members received a copy of
Badger History magazine, a newsletter, a membership card, buttons,
and a chapter charter.[21] Dues ranged from 25 cents for groups
of five or more to 75 cents for children who were not part of an
organized chapter.[22] Additionally, the Society circulated copies of
the *Wisconsin Teacher Newsletter* to teachers who led junior chapters.

In October 1947, the Society published the first issue of the
monthly *Badger History*. The magazine featured brief articles on
people and events in Wisconsin's past written by Society staff and
other experts, as well as articles written by schoolchildren. The
magazine also printed suggestions detailing how children could
be historians themselves by preserving objects, reading appropriate history books, or visiting historic places. The magazine had two
distinct sections, one aimed at elementary grades and the other at
the intermediate grades.[23] Editors of *Badger History* connected with

Wisconsin's outstanding junior historians are honored at the Wisconsin
State Capitol in 1957. With them on the back row, left to right, are Clifford
Lord, Society director; Governor Vernon Thomson; and Thurman Fox,
the Society's chief of school services.

children by promising that "this new BADGER HISTORY magazine is yours. . . . Our magazine will be written FOR you and BY you. We shall print your stories, essays, poems, histories, pictures, hobbies, cartoons—all about your community, your county, your state."[24]

Enthusiasm for Wisconsin history ran high with the statehood centennial only a year away. Yet little could Society staff have known how popular the junior program would be. In December 1947, the junior historian program operated 102 chapters and had almost 2,000 members.[25] By the end of the program's first year, membership grew to more than 14,000 students.[26] The junior chapters were active on a number of projects. Several chapters wrote histories of their school districts or of notable farms in their area, while others wrote about local churches or cemeteries.[27]

Chapter members often wrote to the editors of *Badger History* to tell of their achievements. A chapter in Waupaca reported that they were helping with a Danish Waupaca program, including compiling a cookbook and holding a literary benefit program.[28] Another chapter reported, perhaps with a bit of hyperbole: "We also made a complete study of Wisconsin, learning everything we possibly could about it."[29] At the conclusion of the first year of the program, Lord reported proudly: "The activities of our juniors would quite literally fill a book."[30]

A decade later, Wisconsin had one of the most active junior historian programs in the nation.[31] Membership had grown to 20,687 students in 1,156 chapters.[32] The director of the junior historian program noted with pride that in the first decade of its existence, *Badger History* had printed 1,100 articles written by schoolchildren.[33] Growth in the students was also palpable, as the program director wrote: "The past is tied to the present in the child's mind as he finds, through interviewing and reading and writing, that history is real and alive."[34] The Society encouraged junior chapters by awarding prizes for group projects, essays, models of historic buildings, oratory and audiovisual projects, posters, murals, and scrapbooks.[35] Up to six conventions were held at different locations in the state, drawing thousands of children to see skits and pageants or tour historic sites.[36] Young people were increasingly making their own history. Students interviewed grandparents for special projects, rescuing stories that may have been forever lost; they sometimes found antiques and historic objects when visiting older people to talk about earlier times. Some young historians borrowed objects to create a museum in their schools, which developed an interest in history throughout the community.[37] By 1960, the Society regularly fielded questions from several states seeking advice on how to start a similar program.[38]

At the same time, the Society connected with school children and communities using one of its most distinctive and popular venues, the Historymobile. The Historymobile consisted of a Ford pickup and a mobile home modified to host Museum exhibits.[39] In April 1954, the Historymobile set out from Madison on its first tour of Wisconsin, bringing an exhibit titled *History through Our Historic Sites*.[40] For more than two decades, the Society sent a new traveling exhibit on the road for up to 230 days each year, parking at schools and village halls where residents would line up to walk through exhibits with titles such as *Wisconsin: Wilderness, Territory, Frontier State; Sawdust and Spangles: The Circus in Wisconsin*; and *Signers of the Declaration of Independence*. The Society printed study guides for the exhibits, one version for students and another for

The Society's Historymobile brought displays and artifacts to communities around the state, beginning in the mid-1950s and continuing until the late 1970s.

teachers. Society staff members were on hand to answer questions and interpret the exhibits.

No admission was charged to view the traveling museum. Visitors saw firsthand the objects and documents that formed part of the raw material of the history of the state. A visit from the Historymobile was a special event for most communities. The local papers would announce its impending arrival, and families toured its exhibits with great enthusiasm. During its twenty-three-year existence, the Historymobile would travel almost eighty thousand miles and host three million people.[41]

The Press, which had faltered throughout the Depression years, also saw substantial changes in the mid-twentieth century. Significantly, Lord recruited distinguished editor Livia Appel from the University of Wisconsin Press. Eminent historian William Hesseltine once wrote that Appel's "high standards, critical insights, and unconquerable zeal for perfection, have, through many years, tutored my laggard pen."[42] Over the next eight years under Appel's watch, the Press produced "the most distinguished shelf of publications ever to appear over the Society's imprimatur."[43] A closer relationship with the University of Wisconsin in the postwar era also sparked the creation of Logmark Editions, an imprint of the Press that published notable theses written by University of Wisconsin students.

Other changes were afoot. In 1953, the university library moved into the new Memorial Library on the block next to the Wisconsin Historical Society.[44] Society collections promptly filled the vacated space, as construction crews began an extensive renovation of the building's interior.

The renovation effectively doubled the size of the Museum, as additional galleries on the first floor were cleared to make way for Museum exhibits. The Library's shelving space expanded by forty percent, and fifty study carrels were created in the stacks for graduate students. That same year, the Society donated one hundred thousand books and pamphlets from its non-American materials to Memorial Library.[45] The Society continued to serve as the university's North American research collection, a role the Library still fulfills today.

Austin E. Quinney was a leader in the Stockbridge tribe's move from New York to Wisconsin in the 1820s. Quinney helped negotiate a series of treaties to secure and protect land for the tribe, who were under constant threat of dispossession. Dr. Amos C. Hamlin Jr. painted this portrait of Quinney in 1849. This is image is one of about 50,000 contained in the Society's portrait files and is one of hundreds of original paintings owned by the Society.

These garters, in the Museum's collections, are the same finger-woven garters worn by Austin E. Quinney for his portrait.

THE FIRST HISTORIC SITES

Around this time, a new trend in museum design began to take root: the historic site. Originally conceived in the nineteenth century as a way to display artifacts in a historically rich environment, historic sites in the early twentieth century evolved into places where people could experience "a feeling of historical mood, a haunting impression of having passed this way before."[46]

For much of the twentieth century, automobiles helped Wisconsin's economy grow, creating jobs in manufacturing and tourism. State and local governments improved roads, while resort owners and small-town boosters sent out promotional materials to attract travelers by showing the many recreations available just off Wisconsin's highways. Responding to this progress, the Society originally began exploring the possibility of acquiring historic sites in the 1940s, when the post–World War II generation sought destinations for day trips and places to visit while on vacation. But in the early 1950s, the planning finally came to fruition with the Society's first three Historic Sites: Villa Louis, Wade House, and Stonefield.

Villa Louis is an Italianate mansion built on Saint Feriole Island on the Mississippi River. In the 1830s, a trader named Hercules Dousman acquired the island from the US government, which formerly tried to operate a fort on the oft-flooded parcel of land. Dousman built an elegant home on a bluff on the island, in a spot that did not flood. After his death, the property passed to his son Louis, who in 1870 tore down his father's original home, recycled some of the materials, and constructed a new residence in the Italian villa style. In 1885, he added stables, barns, a racetrack, and other buildings and remodeled the interior of the villa to embody the principles of the British arts and crafts movement. A reaction against industrialization and machine-produced goods, the arts and crafts movement emphasized simple ornamentation, quality materials, and traditional construction techniques. Louis Dousman died shortly after the 1885 renovation at only thirty-seven years old. The villa stood empty for several years when Louis's widow remarried and moved east.

In the 1930s, descendants of Hercules and Louis Dousman renovated the villa and offered the property to the Wisconsin Historical Society. The Society passed; at the time, it was struggling to weather the Depression. So the city of Prairie du Chien operated the home as a museum. As the Society began its post-Depression rebirth, the Dousman heirs once again negotiated with the Society to transfer ownership of the villa. On January 1, 1950, the Society finally acquired the title to the property. Two years later, in April 1952, Villa Louis opened to the public as the Society's first Historic Site. Subsequent donations and purchases of Dousman family papers, photographs, furnishings, and accessories original to the house helped preserve the story of the villa and would aid a major restoration of the estate that would begin in 1994.

Even as the Society worked to acquire Villa Louis, plans were in the works to acquire Wade House, built in Greenbush in 1850 by Sylvanus Wade. This three-story Greek-revival stagecoach inn grew to be a regular stopping point and meeting place. It was the scene of countless cotillions and caucuses, a place for locals and travelers to mingle and discuss the issues of the day. With the construction of a new road between Sheboygan and Fond du Lac, the bustling village of Greenbush seemed to have a bright future. However, little more than a decade later, Greenbush was bypassed by the railroad, and the inevitable decline of the once-ascendant town began.

Painting by Cal Peters depicting the battle of Bad Axe at the Wisconsin River on August 2, 1832

The Dousman family
and friends on the
east porch of Villa
Louis, ca. 1898

Interior view of the front hallway of Villa Louis

Wade House remained in business until 1910, then served as a private residence until 1941, when the owners sold it to a family friend who planned to restore the house. When money ran out in 1950, the owners sold Wade House to Marie Kohler, daughter of Kohler Company founder John Michael Kohler, and her sister-in-law Ruth DeYoung Kohler. The Kohler family planned a three-year, top-to-bottom restoration of the old inn. Marie died before the restoration began, and the work was ably directed by Ruth, who wished to deed the property to the Society upon completion of the project. Sadly, Ruth died three months shy of the grand opening, at age forty-six. On June 6, 1953, with poet Carl Sandburg on hand, Wade House opened to the public.

In the following years, the Society would make additions to the grounds of Wade House. The Wesley W. Jung Carriage House Museum opened to the public in 1968, displaying the handiwork of several carriage makers. In 1999, builders and craftsmen constructed a replica of the Herrling Sawmill, which stood near the inn in the late nineteenth century. The mill can be operated using water power or with the help of a motor when water is low.

Wade House, built in Greenbush in 1850

Not long after the opening of Wade House, the Society began operating Stonefield, a site north of Cassville that was once the home of Wisconsin's first governor, Nelson Dewey. In 1836, Dewey moved to Wisconsin Territory to practice law. He also worked to build the village of Cassville on the Mississippi River, believing it would one day be a major city. After completing his two terms as governor, Dewey turned his attention, and his not-inconsiderable fortune, toward Cassville's development, including the construction of a mansion on two thousand acres of land near the Mississippi River. But Dewey lost most of his fortune in the panic of 1873, and the same year, his beloved mansion burned to the ground. A few years later, the property was sold, and a modest summer residence was built on the foundations of Dewey's incinerated mansion. In 1936, the State of Wisconsin purchased the land and buildings.

A visitor to Stonefield gets a firsthand look at a blacksmith's work.

In 1953, the legislature designated Stonefield as the state's farm and craft museum, and on July 4, 1953, Stonefield opened to the public. Using modest funding granted by the legislature, the Society and the local government began collecting artifacts and farm implements for the site. By the end of the 1950s, the Society had constructed more than thirty buildings to make up Stonefield Village, offering visitors a historic view of farm life in rural Wisconsin. The site's assortment of antique farm implements and machinery grew rapidly, prompting construction of a new home for Stonefield's agricultural collections. In 1971, the Society constructed a building on the foundations of Dewey's original sheep barn and opened it as the State Agricultural Museum. Today it houses Wisconsin's largest collection of farm tools, models, and machinery detailing the state's agricultural past. Stonefield enlightens visitors about turn-of-the-century technology, the agricultural community that cultivated Wisconsin's growth, and the colorful characters who helped make the state into "America's Dairyland."

All of these changes, and the impressive growth they inspired, came from Clifford Lord's commitment to his grand vision for a new era, in which the Society would be of "greatly increased utility both to the scholar and to the people of Wisconsin."[47] He did this by strengthening relationships with schools and communities, re-energizing struggling and long-dormant programs, and laying the foundation for a rich network of historic sites, engaging Wisconsinites from almost every background and corner of the state.

And yet, in 1958, Clifford Lord reluctantly resigned as director to become dean of the School of General Studies at Columbia University. While the deanship was an opportunity Lord relished, and it allowed him to return to his roots in New York, he left Wisconsin with great regret. Lord, in large effect, rebuilt the Society and, in the process, developed a strong filial affection for the institution and the people of Wisconsin. Yet Lord felt the time was right to leave, "to give the Lady a new consort for the promising era that lies ahead."[48]

Chapter Five

—— ‖ ——

THE GRAND OLD
LADY'S NEW ERA
1950s–1980s

By the time of Clifford Lord's departure, the Society had grown into an intricate organization no longer bound by the walls of its headquarters building in Madison. Its "Old West" days were in the past as a professional staff of librarians, archivists, editors, curators, and administrators ably ran the Society. While subsequent directors have provided essential leadership and vision, the Society moved into the 1960s and '70s with the newfound flexibility and depth of knowledge, embodied in its professional staff, essential for meeting the challenges the new technical age would bring.

A series of administrative changes in the 1960s helped the Society function more efficiently and provide more services to more people around the state. Under the leadership of director Les Fishel, the Society's manuscript collections, state archives, and iconographic collections were merged into a new Archives division. Fishel also created an Office of Local History, an Editorial Division, and the new position of State Archaeologist. Meanwhile, the Society budget more than doubled during this decade. Society staff grew from 88 to 128, and membership increased from 4,300 to 6,500. Several historic sites were added to the fold under Fishel's leadership, while an addition to the Society's headquarters building helped the Museum gain visibility with first floor galleries. All the while, the Society was adapting to new technologies and documenting the many social changes then sweeping America.

Using New Media

As technology gave birth to new broadcast media throughout the twentieth century, the Society eagerly embraced these new forms to share history. As early as the 1930s, Society staff had used the radio as a way to reach out to the public.[1] Charles Brown of the Museum staff and Louise P. Kellogg, a researcher, writer, and historian who worked in the Society Library, both appeared on WHA radio, with Brown making nine appearances on the station in 1932. Ten years later, Society director Edward Alexander gave a course of thirty-two lectures on Wisconsin history over the two state radio stations then broadcasting, WHA in Madison and WLBL in Stevens Point.[2] The centennial of Wisconsin's statehood in 1948 revived interest in history, and Society staff made regular appearances for radio interviews. By the 1950s, Society staff used radio to lend expertise to local history groups, broadcasting talks by experts over FM radio and facilitating book discussions and study groups that followed assignments and lectures delivered over the airwaves by Society experts.

In the 1950s, the Society also began to create television programs. In 1953, the Society launched a twenty-seven-minute color film, *The Presence of Our Past*, which documented the wide-ranging activities of the Society. With the advent of WHA-TV, the state's public television station, the Society began to work with the new station to produce several programs, including a panel quiz show, *TV Museum*; fifteen children's programs, including *Grandma's Attic*; and numerous five-minute short programs.[3] On *Lori's Log Cabin*, a program for children that aired on public television in the 1960s, a Society staffer played the role of a new settler in early Wisconsin who would ask other settlers for advice and help.

Throughout the 1960s, the Society remained active in radio and television. Society staff created hundreds of programs for radio and television, including a public television series titled *Wisconsin Windows* that covered topics ranging from the Civil War centennial to the Society-run Historic Sites. For several years, Society staff produced a series on Wisconsin writers, while special programs for radio and television were regularly recorded in and around

Society staff members working on a show with WHA-TV

the Society's headquarters building.[4] The Society hired a staff pro-
gramming coordinator who worked on scripts, recorded radio and
television programs, and traveled around the state filming historic
sites and other notable locations for use in broadcast programs.[5]

DOCUMENTING SOCIAL MOVEMENTS

In the 1960s, under the leadership of Les Fishel, the Society made
the conscious decision to document controversial aspects of contemporary history including the struggle over Civil Rights and the
anti-Vietnam war movement.

Since the turn of the twentieth century, the Society had documented some of the most pressing issues facing the country. As
the culture evolved, so too did the Society's efforts to document
changes. In this way, the work to document socialism, communism,
Social Security and entitlements evolved into work documenting
civil liberties and free speech. Where the Society's attention was
focused on organizations such as the International Workingman's
Association and Milwaukee's Socialist congressman Victor Berger,
in the 1960s the focus changed to the Congress of Racial Equality

and Civil Rights advocates like Daisy Bates and Amzie Moore. At the same time, the longstanding work of documenting organized labor was updated and included in this national effort.

Just one example of the numerous movements documented in the Society's collections was the work to gather the records of Mississippi Freedom Summer. In the summer of 1964, more than sixty thousand black residents of Mississippi risked their lives to vote, aiming to break the power of the segregated Democratic Party and, in the process, break down segregation in the South. Aiding these efforts were nonviolent activists, many from northern states, who traveled across Mississippi registering black voters. On the first day of the voter registration efforts, activists Andrew Goodman, James Chaney, and Michael Schwerner were kidnapped and killed by white supremacists. The story of their activism and their murders formed the storyline for the 1988 film *Mississippi Burning*.

Several Society field workers traveled across the South, amassing more than one hundred thousand pages of documents such as letters, diaries, newspaper clippings, photos, memos, and much more. The Society's collection of Freedom Summer documents

is the only collection gathered on the ground from grassroots activists during the 1960s, while the Civil Rights struggle was still unfolding. Years later, to commemorate Freedom Summer's fiftieth anniversary, the Society Press published a compilation of many of these documents in a volume titled *Risking Everything: A Freedom Summer Reader*, edited by Michael Edmonds, from the Society's Library-Archives division. In 2014, Society staff

A mother and child hold signs opposing school segregation in Milwaukee, ca. 1964.

created a traveling exhibit for a year-long journey through Milwaukee-area schools, libraries, and museums, sharing the inspiring stories behind Freedom Summer and the people who made it possible.

While the work of documenting many of the movements of the 1950s and 60s had a national focus, similar social movements in Wisconsin have not escaped the Society's attention. The Society holds the key records of Father James Groppi, a Milwaukee native and Roman Catholic priest who gained national attention for his work in the Civil Rights movement and the Milwaukee open housing movement. The Society also holds the papers of Milwaukee Alderperson Vel Phillips, who repeatedly introduced open housing legislation as a member of Milwaukee's Common Council, and who went on to become the first African American judge in Wisconsin, as well as the first woman judge in Milwaukee County. In 1968, while still a Milwaukee Alder, Phillips saw the Common

One of the many compelling images from the Society's Freedom Summer collection. Here, two men holding protest signs walk past a white police officer with a bullhorn during a Greenwood, Mississippi, Freedom Day. In the background a police vehicle is parked at the curb. The Society Press's book, *Risking Everything: A Freedom Summer Reader*, published in 2014, commemorates Freedom Summer's fiftieth anniversary.

Council pass a desegregation law, six years after she introduced open housing legislation.

The Society's efforts to document social movements have continued to evolve. The work accomplished in the 1960s set the foundation for the Society to document later social movements, such as the abortion rights debate, the efforts to oppose American involvement in Central America in the 1980s, and the off-reservation spearing debates in the 1980s and 1990s.

History for Everyone

In 1962, to make its rich collection of archival sources available to researchers throughout the state, the Society began to convert several government document repositories on university campuses around Wisconsin into active research centers. This was the start of the Society's Area Research Center system, which has grown into a statewide network of archival collections stored at thirteen UW campus libraries and the Northern Great Lakes Visitor Center outside of Ashland.[6]

Each research center serves a specific geographic region and houses records created in, and focused on, that region. This system makes the collections much more accessible. Today, the Society's Area Research Center system leads the nation in the size, scope, and usage of its network. UW campuses provide staff to help users navigate collections and a courier system allows the centers to share materials, while the Society enables campuses to provide access to primary documents for undergraduates, high school students, and university faculty.

Preserving State Heritage

The increased mobility and prosperity of the post-World War II era that facilitated the Historic Sites and Area Research Centers came with a price. Urban renewal and interstate highway projects threatened historically significant places and inspired preservationists to take action. By this time, it was clear that not every historic structure, place, or neighborhood could be owned and operated by a single organization. While the Society's early history focused on owning historic resources—books, manuscripts, and artifacts, not to mention the Historic Sites the Society continued adding to its collections—the Society realized it needed to find new ways for other people and groups to participate in preserving the state's heritage. The historic preservation movement of the second half of the twentieth century ultimately enabled the Society to share tools and incentives with individuals and interested groups to preserve their own properties.

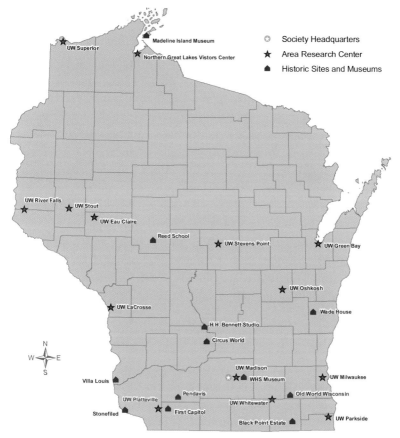

This map shows the locations of Society's fourteen Area Research Centers and twelve Historic Sites.

As in other states around the nation, Wisconsin's first steps in historic preservation were taken by private groups and individuals. In 1903, people concerned about preserving Wisconsin's Native American artifacts and sites founded the Wisconsin Archaeological Society. By the 1920s, the group had helped save five hundred Indian mounds throughout the state. In 1908, the Wisconsin Federation of Women's Clubs partnered with the Wisconsin Archaeological Society and the Sauk County Historical Society to purchase Man Mound near Baraboo, the only surviving human effigy mound in the United States. Other projects typically involved the purchase of historically significant buildings, such as the Old Agency House and Fort Winnebago in Portage, the Little White Schoolhouse in Ripon, Saint Augustine Church in New Diggings, and historic Hazelwood in Green Bay, the home of the principal author of Wisconsin's constitution. A significant legislative step toward preservation came when Wisconsin enacted the Integrated Park Act in 1947, which made it possible for the state to purchase, restore, and develop properties of historic and archaeological significance. The first property purchased under this legislation in 1952 was a portion of the one-thousand-year-old site of Aztalan.

The same federal legislation that created the interstate highway system in 1956 provided for the protection and recovery of historic, archaeological, and paleontological resources. Although the act did not mandate state compliance with these provisions, Wisconsin's Highway Department nonetheless created a procedure to allow limited archaeological research before highway construction. Federal law also required each state to select an institutional sponsor for archaeology. In Wisconsin, that institution was the Society.

The Society has had an interest in archaeology since its very beginnings. Noted scientist Increase Lapham, who served as the Society's first corresponding secretary, offered a resolution in 1849: "That the surveyors throughout this state be requested to furnish this Society with sketches from actual measurements of the ancient mounds and artificial earth-works in their vicinity." In 1879, the Society had its first direct involvement in an archaeological dig when Lyman Draper sent an observer to assist with the exploration of a cave in western Wisconsin that contained Native American petroglyphs. After the turn of the 20th century, Charles E. Brown was the Society's most prominent face of archaeology. While Brown worked to survey and document sites around Wisconsin, he also did some collecting for the Museum.

The Society's archaeological efforts would change with the beginning of the post-World War II historic preservation movement. In 1958, the Society negotiated its first cooperative agreement with the State Highway Commission, which would provide money for field survey and excavation. As a result, the Society improved its ability to tell stories from ancient Wisconsin. A decade of intensive fieldwork made significant progress. For example, archaeologists excavated the Millville site in Grant County and discovered the remains of fourteen Native American circular houses, part of a community that was 1,600 years old.

The success of the highway program led to negotiations with the Department of Natural Resources, which resulted in support for work at Wisconsin's most famous archaeological site, Aztalan. This ancient settlement, dating back to the tenth century, sits along the west bank of the Crawfish River, east of Lake Mills in Jefferson County. Society archaeologists worked at Aztalan for three years focusing on the stockade, the pyramidal mound, and the village area.

In 1966, Congress passed the National Historic Preservation Act, which established state historic preservation offices in every state. It also established the National Register of Historic Places, which defined criteria for determining the importance of a property. These standards have helped make the process of historic preservation more efficient, effective, and accessible.

With the passage of the National Historic Preservation Act, the Society became the federally designated State Historic Preservation Office, an active role that it continues to play today. The Society nominates places of architectural, historic, and archaeological significance to the National Register of Historic Places in partnership with the National Park Service, and it manages the State Register of Historic Places. The Society also reviews federal, state, and local projects for their impact on historic and archaeological properties,

administers state and federal tax credit programs, and runs the
state's burial sites protection program.

The National Historic Preservation Act required that government agencies using federal funds consider archaeological sites
in project development. As a result, the Society began to increase
its archaeological field research on a contract basis with federal
and state agencies. For example, in 1971, funded by the US Army
Corps of Engineers, the Society began the first large-scale archaeological survey ever conducted in the state, known as the La Farge
Reservoir Project. This was a ten-year study to locate archaeological
sites in the Kickapoo River Valley in Vernon County. The La Farge
survey identified more than two hundred archaeological sites, providing the first complete sequence of more than ten thousand
years of human occupation in Wisconsin.

As the Society settled into its role as the State Historic Preservation Office, archaeological efforts branched off into different
directions. Archaeologists with the Society's Historic Preservation
Division worked to document, and thus preserve in some fashion,
historic places around the state. Meanwhile the staff of the Highway Archaeology Salvage Program, which would later be renamed
the Museum Archaeology Program, became more focused on
artifact collections. Additionally, Museum Archaeology Program
staff has, over the past century, developed instructional materials
to help teach Wisconsin history; trained thousands of students,
interns and volunteers in archaeological field methods and techniques, laboratory methods and techniques, and the curation of
archaeological collections; and has curated and managed the
archaeological object collections and associated documentation
owned by the state.

The Society also began providing grants and technical advice
to help communities across the state identify and protect historic
resources. In the 1960s and '70s, local governments began adopt-
ing local historic preservation ordinances and designating local
landmarks and districts. The first community in Wisconsin to develop a historic preservation ordinance and appoint a preservation
commission was Milwaukee in 1963. Madison followed suit in 1970,
Fond du Lac in 1971, and Mineral Point in 1972. As of 2014, a total

of sixty-eight units of local government are working to protect their historic resources with the assistance of the Society.

STRENGTHENING THE HISTORIC SITES

Even as more people and communities were engaged in historic preservation, the Society continued to gather new Historic Sites into its fold. The Society's next four acquisitions represent interest in social history and the lives of ordinary individuals. Each of these— Circus World Museum, Madeline Island Museum, Pendarvis, and Old World Wisconsin—reflects the passion of creative energies during the era, since each was fashioned specifically to tell a story.

Circus World Museum tells the story of Wisconsin's unusually rich circus heritage. In 1884, the five Ringling brothers (Al, Otto, Charles, John, and Alf) founded the circus that still bears their name today. The circus's winter quarters in Baraboo became known to locals as "Ringlingville." Surviving buildings stand along

One of the beautifully restored circus wagons at Circus World

the north bank of the Baraboo River and date from between 1897 and 1916. There are also remnants of a footbridge that employees used to cross the river. This is the largest group of original circus structures in North America.

The Circus World Museum was deeded to the Wisconsin Historical Society the day after it opened on July 1, 1959. Unlike the other sites, this museum is operated by a separate nonprofit corporation. Circus World's original site was less than one acre of land and included the Ringling Camel House and Ring Barn, both of which were acquired in 1957. Over the years, land and structures were added until the site encompassed about sixty-four acres of land with thirty permanent structures, including eight original winter quarters buildings, plus the original Ringling Brothers Circus Train complex.

Circus World's collection of circus artifacts is the largest in the world and includes more than 210 original wagons and vehicles once used by American, English, and Irish circuses. Circus World

Circus World houses more than 8,650 colorful circus posters
in the largest collection of circus artifacts in the world.

houses an exceptional collection of circus ads and posters, with more than 8,650 multicolored circus posters that range in size from half-sheets, or about the size of a newspaper, to a large 80-sheet Buffalo Bill Wild West poster measuring 9 feet high and 70 feet long. The collection also includes thousands of journals, manuscripts, business records, original fine art oil paintings, handbills, programs, costumes, personal artifacts of circus performers, and a collection of rare photographs, motion picture film, and glass-plate negatives.

In 1968, the Society acquired the Madeline Island Museum, located on Lake Superior's Madeline Island, not far from Bayfield. This northernmost of the Society's historic sites was the idea of Leo and Bella Capser, summer residents who opened the museum in 1958. The Capsers worked with archaeologists and local historians, gathering artifacts and local history stories to create their displays. The Museum is located in four historic buildings, including the last remaining building of John Jacob Astor's American Fur

Painting of La Pointe, on Madeline Island, depicting the buildings of the American Fur Company and both of the mission churches, ca. 1842

An interpreter at the Madeline Island Museum shows a pelt to a visiting family.

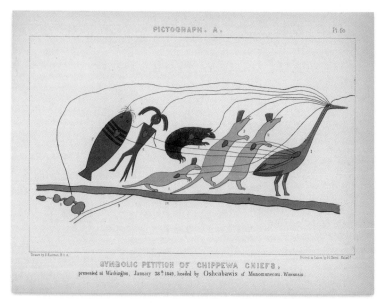

Nineteenth-century petition from Ojibwe clan chiefs. The animal figures represent clan leaders, the thick line represents Lake Superior, and the four small ovals represent rice beds. This petition indicates that the Ojibwe are of one mind and one heart and do not wish to be removed from their wild rice beds near Lake Superior.

Company complex built at La Pointe in 1835, which is the oldest building on Madeline Island. This building adjoins an old barn, the former La Pointe jail, and the Old Sailor's Home, which was built as a memorial to a drowned soldier.

The Society assumed operations in 1968 and expanded the museum in 1991 by adding the Capser Center, which houses rotating exhibits on island and regional history, an auditorium, a museum store, space for storing collections and fabricating exhibits, and staff offices. In 2005, the museum added a Walkway Gallery connecting the Capser Center with the original museum. The museum is fully endowed by private money and uses no state operating funds.

Visitors to Madeline Island Museum can see Native American beaded objects, clothing, and tools, as well as explorer and voyageur artifacts that tell the story of the fur trade. Also on display are tools and equipment used in logging and lumbering, boat building, commercial fishing, carpentry, and barrel making. Objects and photographs inside the barn depict the daily lives of the nineteenth- and early-twentieth-century settlers. Catholic and Protestant missionary history is represented with a unique collection of artifacts and religious books translated into Ojibwe.

In 1970, the Wisconsin Historical Society acquired Pendarvis, a collection of ten structures in Mineral Point that tell the story of Cornish settlement and the heyday of lead mining in Wisconsin. Experienced miners began arriving from Cornwall in southwestern England in the 1830s, settling in Mineral Point and throughout the Upper Mississippi lead region. Here they constructed small limestone homes similar to those they had left in England. Mineral Point became a thriving commercial center, and the boom continued into early Wisconsin statehood when zinc mining and processing became the dominant mining activity.

Almost a hundred years later, local restaurateurs Robert Neal and Edgar Hellum found Mineral Point's history and heritage endangered. Starting in 1935, Neal and Hellum decided to preserve these tangible symbols of Mineral Point's past by acquiring and rehabilitating several original structures. Following the Cornish tradition of giving a name to each house, they called their first

Pendarvis House, one of several houses restored by Robert Neal and Edgar Hellum

restoration Pendarvis, after an estate in Cornwall. They gave the other houses Cornish names, too—Polperro and Trelawny. They created the verdant gardens of Pendarvis in the 1930s to recall those planted by the Cornish settlers upon their arrival in Mineral Point a hundred years earlier. In 1971, the Wisconsin Historical Society acquired Pendarvis, as well as forty acres of land across Shake Rag Street containing the Merry Christmas Mine. Today, Pendarvis is operated as a Historic Site interpreting the history of Cornish settlement and Wisconsin lead mining.

Even before the Society acquired Pendarvis, plans were in the works for an open-air museum dedicated to preserving the quickly-vanishing architecture of Wisconsin's immigrant populations. Old World Wisconsin was the brainchild of Milwaukee architect Richard Perrin, who noted with regret the rapid destruction of the remaining examples of immigrant architecture. Perrin brought his idea for an open-air museum to director Les Fishel in the early 1960s, yet it took most of the decade to build the necessary momentum to create the museum. The Society faced several obstacles, money being the biggest challenge. Even so, Perrin and a few others persisted, and by the end of the decade a team of workers—architects, historians, laborers—had begun one of the largest preservation projects in the nation.

Old World Wisconsin opened in 1976, after many years of planning and collecting. To create this museum, Society researchers traveled throughout Wisconsin in search of authentic historic buildings hewn by earlier generations of settlers. From Lake Superior to the Illinois border, from the Mississippi River to Lake Michigan, historians documented old farmhouses, outbuildings, and small-town structures. Once the research was complete, construction of Old World Wisconsin began. Piece by piece, workers painstakingly dismantled the old structures. They numbered bricks, boards, and logs and moved them to the site of Old World Wisconsin, in the town of Eagle. In a setting largely unchanged from the rolling prairies the first pioneers found, the buildings took shape once again. Old World Wisconsin was a unique project, billed as "the world's multinational, multicultural outdoor museum."[7]

Today, Old World Wisconsin's historic farm and village buildings comprise the world's largest museum dedicated to the history of rural life. More than sixty historic structures range from farmsteads with furnished houses and rural outbuildings to a crossroads village with traditional small-town institutions. Old World is a unique place where visitors can get a hands-on experience of daily life in Wisconsin, whether washing clothes by hand or preparing food in a nineteenth-century kitchen. Plants representative of those grown by Wisconsin pioneers are preserved at Old World, and historic animal breeds give visitors a glimpse of the types of animals that shared in the work of, and sometimes became the food for, Wisconsin's pioneers. Visitors can watch draft horses working the fields, a team of oxen pulling their load, sheep getting shorn, and flocks of chickens just like those found on every Wisconsin farm.

The hardworking oxen at Old World Wisconsin in Eagle
are a perennial favorite with visitors.

The Kruza house at Old World Wisconsin is an example of a Polish
farmstead from the late nineteenth century. It is an example of stovewood
construction, a European building technique in which logs are cut into
short, uniform sections and stacked to resemble piles of firewood.

A Changing Library and Archives

The 1970s saw a dramatic shift in the clientele served by the Library and Archives. The Civil War centennial in the 1960s and the bicentennial of the American Revolution in 1976 awakened many Americans to their own family history, bringing amateur researchers to the Library and Archives in greater numbers.[8] For most of the twentieth century, the lion's share of the Library's users had been students and scholars; but by the late 1970s, genealogists made up half of the Library's patrons.[9] Students and amateur researchers competed with one another for seats in the reading room, while researchers wanting a vacant microfilm reader needed to arrive as soon as the doors opened.[10]

By the mid-1970s, the Library had a staff of twenty-nine; but the economic downturn following the 1974 oil embargo ultimately led to the elimination of four positions, even as demands on staff were increasing. Many of the new genealogists using the Library had no experience navigating primary documents, so staff began teaching classes and publicizing the Society's genealogical collections.[11] Catalogers worked to reclassify books from the old Cutter-based system, while the collection of contemporary materials—newspapers, pamphlets, and newsletters, among other items—increased dramatically. Even as these changes took place, the Library's catalog was moving into the computer age. Thus, from the end of the 1970s through the 1990s, greater integration of the Society and university's electronic catalogs, and their increased availability, brought more students and researchers to the Society Library. With these increased demands on staff, the Library depended increasingly on student help, volunteers, and, for a short time, first offenders sentenced to community service to handle tasks such as shelving and dusting the Library stacks.

Publishing "World Treasures"

Likewise, the Press, with a staff of only five, labored to produce half a dozen books each year, publish *Wisconsin Magazine of History* each quarter, create an annual catalog, generate mailing lists, and promote their books whenever possible. A former editor from the time recalled that the editors "periodically hauled [books] to historical conventions in places as distant as New York and Washington in the society's station wagon."

Yet the Press managed to publish an impressive collection of titles in the 1970s and '80s, including five of the six volumes of the *History of Wisconsin* series. Society director Les Fishel announced the project at the beginning of the planning phase in 1960. This history of the state would begin with the earliest times and stretch up to the modern day, with each four-hundred-page volume to encompass a significant period in

Les Fishel, Society director from 1959 to 1969

Wisconsin's development: volume 1, *From Exploration to Statehood*; volume 2, *The Civil War Era*; volume 3, *Urbanization and Industrialization*; volume 4, *The Progressive Era*; volume 5, *War, a New Era, and Depression*; and volume 6, *Continuity and Change*. The *History of Wisconsin* ultimately involved six authors and dozens of researchers. The first volume was published in 1973, just in time for the farewell party for the volume's distinguished author, Alice E. Smith. Twenty-five years later, the final volume was published, coincidentally during Wisconsin's sesquicentennial year.

In 1976, the Press published the first books in another series that continues to this day, the *Documentary History of the Ratification of the Constitution*, a flagship project of the National Historical Records and Publications Commission. Upon publication of the first two volumes of this series in May 1976, Society director James Morton Smith, along with the Press director and several of the series editors, traveled to Washington, DC, to present copies to Warren Burger, then Chief Justice of the Supreme Court.[12] The Press has since published twenty-two more volumes and has several more volumes in development. Following in the tradition of documentary publishing established by Lyman Draper, the series is a standard reference work used by judges and constitutional historians nationwide and has garnered rare praise, being called "the most important editorial project in the nation" as well as "a world treasure."

THE MUSEUM FINDS ITS FOOTING

Although the construction of a T-shaped addition to the headquarters building in 1967 increased the square footage considerably, the Society struggled throughout the 1970s with the perennial problem of overcrowding. In fact, just six years after the addition was built, Society director James Morton Smith wrote that the building "already lacks space for library materials, museum and . . . archival materials."[13] The Museum was especially cramped, still occupying its galleries in the headquarters building. The acquisition of the Historic Sites, especially Old World Wisconsin, had stressed the Society's storage capabilities as items were gathered for eventual use at the sites.

A T-shaped addition to the Society headquarters under construction, 1967

Construction of the addition affected the Museum more than other Society programs. Displays in the first-floor galleries had to be moved occasionally to accommodate the work, and remodeling of the fourth floor substantially reduced the available exhibit space as the gallery was converted into the Archives reading room. One exhibit, a popular display on pharmacy, had stood in

A woman, her son, and a sales clerk are dressed in period costumes in the Museum's pharmacy display.

a fourth-floor gallery for close to sixty years.[14] Even in the midst
of the construction, the Museum opened an exhibit titled "The
Black Community: Its Culture and Heritage" that had been a year
in planning and research.[15] Planning also went forward for future
exhibits celebrating famous Wisconsin women and another about
Philip La Follette, whose papers the Society made available to the
public in the summer of 1970.[16]

An inventory of its collections found that the Museum held
about fifty thousand objects, and even more items were anticipated with the opening of Old World Wisconsin in 1976.[17] Auster-
ity delayed movement on a solution to overcrowding until the late
1970s, when a long-range planning report identified the Society's
major need as "space for the continued growth and proper care
of the collections."[18] The Society began to search for a building
where the Museum could move, to alleviate overcrowding at the
headquarters building.

Finally on July 18, 1980, under the leadership of Director Richard Erney, the Society purchased a vacant building on the Capitol
Square in Madison that was the longtime home of the Wolff, Kubly,
and Hirsig hardware store. Over the next several years the Society renovated the building to house Museum exhibits, fabrication
space, a theatre, a museum store, and a classroom.[19] Despite budgetary constraints, the Museum relocated to Capitol Square in
1986 and has called the location home since. The move helped
temporarily ease storage problems at the headquarters building
and gave the Museum 17,500 square feet of exhibition galleries.
Even with this greatly expanded space, fewer than three percent
of the museum's collections were on exhibit. Through displays
titled *People of the Woodlands, Frontier Wisconsin, The Immigrant State,
Making a Living, Sense of Community,* and *The Political Arena,* visitors
to the Museum today can learn about the history and shared experiences of the many cultures that settled Wisconsin.

Chapter Six

MODERN TIMES
1980s–2010s

Today's Wisconsin Historical Society has gone through several distinct phases in its long history. Like Lyman Draper, who worked so studiously to build a world-class Library, the Society still collects widely the manuscripts, photographs, objects, and stories that document the ongoing evolution of our state and country. Like Reuben Gold Thwaites, who sought to turn the Society into a vehicle for public education, the Society today is active in schools across Wisconsin, creating history curriculum and engaging young historians in the National History Day program. It also maintains an active presence on radio and television and in speaking engagements across the state. Like Edward Alexander and Clifford Lord, who helped the Society more nimbly respond to twentieth-century social and industrial advancements, the Society today works to adapt to the ever-changing technological landscape while meeting the expectations of the diverse people it serves.

THE LIBRARY AND ARCHIVES

Since the 1980s, technology has played an increasingly vital role in the oldest of the Society's undertakings: the Library. As the Library and Archives entered the computer age in the 1980s, Library users' expectations began to shift. The initiation of a campus-wide computerized catalog in the mid-1980s brought students to the Library looking not for esoteric tomes or primary documents but for information often concerning current events.[1] When the Library's catalog became available over the Internet in 1993, researchers around the country and the world discovered the extent of the Society's collections. Society staff began fielding more and more calls from Hollywood writers, fact-checkers at national news outlets such as CNN, and attorneys arguing cases in courtrooms across country.[2] Library patrons were no longer just academic historians—they were customers in a nationwide information marketplace.[3]

In 1997, the Society launched its website, www.wisconsin history.org. From its humble beginnings, the Society website, now in its fourth generation, has grown to contain a wealth of information already difficult to enumerate. Since 1998, more than 10 million pages from Society collections have been shared on the Web. The Society's website includes almost 300,000 pages from rare books, manuscripts, photographs, and other historical documents; these resources are viewed more than 38,000 times each day. Another 163,000 pages from Society collections appear on University

The Reading Room in the Society's headquarters is a popular spot for students and researchers alike.

of Wisconsin websites, while 6.4 million appear in Google books. Another 3.8 million newspaper pages, with content dating back to the colonial era, have been licensed to commercial firms for use in subscription-only newspaper collections. The Society also sells copies of vital records and images through e-commerce applications. Sales and licensing of the Society's online content generates about $250,000 per year. As the Internet has become a standard tool for researchers and history enthusiasts, the Society's website will only continue to grow.

As government records have increasingly moved to electronic formats, the staff and organization of the Society's Library and Archives have undergone major adaptations. Most significantly, the two divisions were merged in 1999 and reorganized to improve services and operate more efficiently. Over the last decade, an increasing amount of the staff's work has shifted to acquiring, managing, preserving, and providing access to digital content. In coming years, this trend will only accelerate. At the same time, Library and Archives staff will continue to protect and preserve the existing record of Wisconsin and national history found in the many books, photographs, and documents collected over the centuries.

Longtime Society archivist Harry Miller examines Land Office records in the Archives stacks.

In no way could Lyman Draper or Reuben Gold Thwaites, who worked to treasure up handbills, newspapers, letters, and similar ephemera, have anticipated the scope and demands of the digital age and its complex technologies. However, their commitment to the important work of history lives on in the present day, and their spirit infuses the efforts of the librarians and archivists who work to preserve and share the story of this state and its people.

THE MUSEUM AND HISTORIC SITES

Draper's spirit infuses the work in the Wisconsin Historical Museum which he worked to build, as well as the Historic Sites program that evolved from it. Today, the Museum's collections contain more than 110,000 historical objects and about half a million archaeological artifacts documenting the history of Wisconsin, including Native people dating back more than twelve thousand years. The Museum has notable collections in the fields of anthropology, business and technology, costumes, textiles and personal artifacts, domestic life, and political and military life. These collections help visitors understand the important trends and events of daily life within diverse social, ethnic, and religious backgrounds.

In the mid-1990s, the Society again added new Historic Sites to its network, almost twenty years after the opening of Old World Wisconsin. The Society's latest additions have largely been historically significant places, preserved and sustained by the investment of time and resources by enthusiastic, interested people. These buildings were not originally created to be museums, but rather they came into the Society's hands only after their original purpose was completed.

In 1995, Society director H. Nicholas Muller III added the First Capitol to the Society's Historic Sites. First Capitol State Park was originally established in 1924, near the picturesque hamlet of Belmont. There, nearly one hundred years earlier, the first territorial legislature established Wisconsin's territorial government during the fall and winter of 1836. One of the acts of this legislature was to name Madison the capital city, after which many people

An African American variation of a friendship quilt, this necktie quilt was created in 1982 with thirty-six necktie fabrics owned by the membership of Milwaukee's Metropolitan Baptist Church.

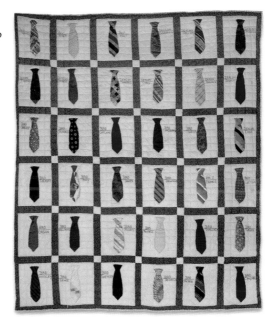

The Milwaukee Braves' first baseman Joe Adcock wore this jersey in 1957.

Part of the original pink flamingo prank by the University of Wisconsin's Pail & Shovel Party, this plastic bird was placed alongside 1,008 other pink flamingos on Bascom Hill on the first day of classes in 1979.

and businesses left Belmont and the surrounding area. The First Capitol site features two buildings used during the 1836 territorial legislative session—the Council House, where the legislators met, and a lodging house. Both structures were eventually used as residences. Initial work to preserve and restore the First Capitol buildings began in the early 1900s, led by the Wisconsin Federation of Women's Clubs. After the Society acquired the buildings in 1995, additional restoration work was done, and First Capitol opened as a Historic Site in 1996.

In 2000, Society director George Vogt presided over the opening of the H. H. Bennett Studio Historic Site in Wisconsin Dells. The studio celebrates the life of Harry Hamilton Bennett, whom experts consider one of the ten best landscape photographers of the nineteenth century. Bennett was one of the first photojournalists using photographs to tell a story. He developed the image of nature as a playground to be enjoyed, not feared, and his stereoscopic views of the Dells attracted visitors from across the country. Bennett embarked on his life as a photographer after a Civil War injury permanently crippled his right hand, preventing him from becoming a carpenter. In 1868, he bought a tintype studio in Wisconsin Dells (then known as Kilbourn City) and took his first stereographic photographs of the rugged Wisconsin River Dells. While other photographers clung to their studios, Bennett developed a passion for landscape photography because, in his words, "It is easier to pose nature and less trouble to please." Bennett constructed all aspects of his cameras except for the lenses. His pioneering use of technology and his exquisite composition skills created an enduring legacy for the Dells, and his photography has hung in some of the most prestigious museums in the world. The Society maintains an extensive collection Bennett's original records and photographs.

In 2007, Society director Ellsworth Brown welcomed Reed School in Neillsville as the Society's tenth Historic Site. Before 1960, most rural Wisconsin children received their education in one-room schools like Reed School. The wide diversity of ages provided opportunities for older students to help their younger peers, an attribute that today's schools find desirable but difficult

Noted Wisconsin photographer H. H. Bennett took this famous photograph of his son Ashley leaping the chasm at Stand Rock, Wisconsin Dells, in 1886. H. H. Bennett's studio is now operated as one of the Society's eleven historic sites.

to achieve. Reed School served as a one-room country school from 1915 to 1951, providing a first- through eighth-grade education. The school is typical of the more than six thousand one-room schools that dotted the landscape of rural Wisconsin. The planners decided to interpret the 1939 school year, replicating interior finishes and wall colors and restoring tin ceilings, plaster walls, and woodwork to their original luster. The Society restored original fixtures and added appropriate period furnishings. The restoration removed decades of overgrowth on the grounds and re-created the original baseball field and outhouse. Like the Madeline Island Museum, the Reed School Historic Site is fully endowed by private money and uses no state operating funds.

The Reed School historic site, near Neillsville, interprets a 1939 one-room schoolhouse.

The Society's most recently added Historic Site is a Victorian summer home in Lake Geneva called Black Point Estate. Lake Geneva has served as a resort community since just after the Civil War, when many wealthy Chicagoans relocated to the area while their homes and places of business were being rebuilt after the Great Chicago Fire of 1871. Many chose to stay there full time, while others built mansions and summer vacation homes there. Chicago brewer Conrad Seipp commissioned Black Point in 1888 as a family summer home. What began as a $20,000, thirteen-bedroom, one-bathroom, twenty-room Queen Anne–style Victorian "cottage" was owned and enjoyed by the same family for 120 years. Today, Black Point Estate has one of the most intact collections of Victorian furnishings found in the Midwest. The property covers nearly eight acres and 620 feet of undisturbed Lake Geneva shoreline.

Black Point Estate Historic House and Gardens, the Society's newest historic site

The Historic Sites attract visitors with a full schedule of activities. When Villa Louis hosts the annual Carriage Classic, the largest competitive carriage-driving competition in the Midwest, the grounds come alive with beautiful horses and fine carriages. Drivers take part in challenges ranging from navigating obstacles to preparing their vehicles for a country picnic while dressed in historic clothes. Because Villa Louis is the site of Wisconsin's only War of 1812 engagement, it also hosts a reenactment of the Battle of Prairie du Chien. And the Breakfast in a Victorian Kitchen event allows participants to experience a Victorian breakfast using the foods, utensils, and technology of the time.

The Villa Louis Carriage Classic is a pleasure-driving show held on the beautiful grounds of the historic site in Prairie du Chien. The Carriage Classic hosts one of the finest carriage-driving competitions in the Midwest.

For more than twenty years, Wade House has hosted a Civil War weekend, complete with sutler's tents and a reenactment of a Civil War battle. Food naturally plays a part in activities at several Historic Sites, including Old World Wisconsin's annual dinner theaters and Wade House's Hearthside Dinner, where attendees experience the ambience of the 1860s stagecoach inn and a meal prepared from authentic historical recipes.

Similarly, the Museum holds events celebrating various facets of Wisconsin life, including music, beer, and quilting. The Museum's popular History Sandwiched In program is an informal brown-bag, lunch-and-lecture series that covers a breadth of historical subjects. The Taste Traditions of Wisconsin program, begun in the early 2000s, explores the rich culinary history, indigenous ingredients, and remarkable ethnic foodways of Wisconsin. Taste Traditions events pair noteworthy speakers with delicious meals, creating a unique experience for Museum visitors. These events are routinely sold out.

At Old World Wisconsin, players recreate the popular 1860s game of vintage base ball, complete with the original styles, rules, and terminology. It's not only a competitive game but also a reenactment of baseball life, similar to an American Civil War reenactment. Vintage base ball is a fast-growing sport in the United States, with 225 clubs in 32 states.

The Sites and the Museum have been a resource for films and documentaries over the years. In 1990, Old World Wisconsin was transformed into a set for the made-for-TV movie *Dillinger*, starring Mark Harmon, Sherilyn Fenn, and Will Patton, while more recently Circus World provided fifteen circus wagons for the filming of the acclaimed movie *Water for Elephants*. *Antiques Road Show* has made multiple visits to the Society headquarters and historic sites, viewing objects in the Museum collections and featuring H. H. Bennett's rafting series of photographs on a program in 2009. And the Museum gained national exposure in a 2012 episode of the Travel Channel's *Mysteries at the Museum* featuring the twisted engine block from the truck used in the 1970 Sterling Hall bombing on the UW campus.[4]

Each year the Sites and Museum draw in more than 300,000 visitors, and they will continue to be an important resource to connect Wisconsinites to the past. The Museum and Sites offer visitors the unique opportunity to engage their senses: the sight of historic barns, houses, gardens, and beasts of burden toiling in fields in much the same way that oxen and draft horses broke the fields in pioneer Wisconsin; the tastes of food prepared using historic recipes and traditional ingredients and tools, served in an historic setting; the sounds of a game of vintage baseball, exploding musketry, or music performed on an antique piano. One young visitor to Old World Wisconsin

Curator Joe Kapler holds the enormous Potter Knife. The knife, which weighs 31 pounds and measures six feet, eight inches, was presented to Wisconsin congressman John Potter by members of the Missouri Republican Party in 1860, after Potter stood up for an antislavery representative from Illinois.

Historical gardeners at Old World Wisconsin plant heirloom varieties of flowers
and vegetables like the ones pictured here to re-create early settler gardens.

was so moved by her experience that she wrote to Old World's director to thank him, stating that her "favorite part (though I had so many) was probably getting to act like a child from the 1800s farm life." The Historic Sites share the sights, sounds and tastes of times gone by, representing a "new and powerful motivation in teaching history to the public."[5]

Involvement in Schools

In the 1990s, the Society revived its earlier commitment to public education. In 1991, at the urging of local historical societies, the state legislature approved funding for expanding the Society's school services program. As a result, the Society developed new tools to assist schools in the teaching of Wisconsin history, including training, workshops, and new curricula. Today, tens of thousands of students visit the Museum and Historic Sites every year.

In the 1990s, the Wisconsin Historical Society Press renewed its efforts to publish quality books for young readers. Working with the school services staff, the Press introduced the New Badger History series, which covered topics in Wisconsin history such as immigration, archaeology, and land use in a format appropriate for elementary- to middle school-aged students. The Press also produced teacher guides, which made the books more useful and accessible for Wisconsin classrooms. These books were the fore-runners of two additional projects that would see light in the early part of the twenty-first century: the Badger Biographies series and *Wisconsin: Our State, Our Story*, the Press's fourth-grade textbook.

The Badger Biographies series started in 2005 with the publi-cation of *Mai Ya's Long Journey*. The book recounts the story of a young Hmong woman whose parents fled Laos during the Viet-nam War, and it follows Mai Ya from her childhood in Thailand's Ban Vinai refugee camp to her new home in Wisconsin. The Bad-ger Biographies series now numbers more than twenty titles and introduces young readers to a diverse set of lives, from famous Wisconsinites Curly Lambeau and Les Paul to lesser-known cit-izens such as Casper Jaggi, a Swiss cheese maker from Monroe, and Kate Pelham Newcomb, a medical doctor in Minocqua in the early to mid-twentieth century. Badger Biographies have been used in elementary classrooms as well as adult literacy programs across the state.

Wisconsin: Our State, Our Story is a full-color, comprehensive textbook presenting Wisconsin history to fourth graders with the "Thinking Like a Historian" method, an inquiry-based method showing students how to investigate the past by asking questions. Artifacts, documents, and vintage photographs illustrate the text-book, giving students a window into the past and the people, buildings, and objects that comprised Wisconsin in former times, while the lessons align with crosscurricular Wisconsin Model Aca-demic Standards. To reach the state's growing Latino population, the Press partnered with Milwaukee Public Schools to create a Spanish-language edition of the textbook, *Wisconsin: Nuestro Es-tado, Nuestra Historia*.

The Society's Junior Historian program flourished until changes to Wisconsin's school system in the 1960s put an end to this promising effort. As early as 1963, membership was declin-ing, in part caused by school consolidation.[6] Fewer teachers were inclined to invest time outside of the classroom to the project after consolidation, and larger schools provided more clubs to

Wisconsin, Our State, Our Story, the Society's fourth-grade history textbook, was produced by the Wisconsin Historical Society Press in both English and Spanish versions.

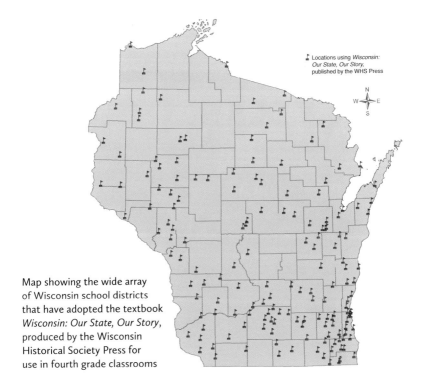

Map showing the wide array of Wisconsin school districts that have adopted the textbook *Wisconsin: Our State, Our Story*, produced by the Wisconsin Historical Society Press for use in fourth grade classrooms

students, which also chipped away at membership.[7] More problematic were the new guidelines for teaching social studies that most school districts adopted in the fall of 1965.[8] These guidelines moved Wisconsin history from middle school grades to the fourth grade, which rendered obsolete much of the material available in *Badger History*.[9]

The Junior Historian program foreshadowed a similar effort that the Society joined in 2001: National History Day. National History Day has become one of the most fruitful venues through which the Society engages younger audiences. Through National History Day in Wisconsin, students in grades six through twelve are given a topic to research by examining historical issues, ideas, people, and events. Students then present their research through exhibits, performances, documentaries, websites, and research papers. These presentations are judged at regional events, with winners advancing to the statewide competition in Madison. From these, a select number of participants are chosen to represent Wisconsin at National History Day's national competition, held

It's obvious which state these National History Day participants are representing!

each summer at the University of Maryland in College Park. Almost 2,000 students participated in the program in its first year, with the help of 41 teachers.[10] During the 2011–2012 academic year, participation grew to 9,000 students and 229 teachers at 103 different schools.[11]

National History Day helps students develop skills in research, writing, critical thinking, and creative expression.[12] Moreover, students become aware of how relevant the past is to their modern lives. In the words of one National History Day participant: "History will never be just words on a page now that I have had the opportunity to do my own research through National History Day. It is a story that continues through everyone's lives and paves the way for the future."[13]

THE WISCONSIN HISTORICAL SOCIETY PRESS

Over the past quarter century, the Wisconsin Historical Society Press has worked to engage larger audiences while maintaining high standards of scholarship in the process. Each year the Press publishes about fourteen titles on an assortment of topics such as architecture and preservation, sports and pastimes, cooking and foodways, popular culture, biography, memoir, and military history. The Press also produces the quarterly *Wisconsin Magazine of History,* which recently won the Award of Merit from the American Association of State and Local History Leadership in History Awards.

The Press has developed strong relationships with other organizations to develop content and promote titles, which has led to an increasing number of books covering a diverse swath of Wisconsin history and culture. Recently the Press partnered with the Oneida Tribe of Indians of Wisconsin to create *A Nation within a Nation: Voices of the Oneidas in Wisconsin,* with the Wisconsin Milk Marketing Board on *Creating Dairyland,* and with the Special Olympics of Wisconsin and Wisconsin's Board for People with Developmental Disabilities to publish and promote *Cindy Bentley: Spirit of a Champion,* to name just a few. Wisconsin Public Television has been an active partner with the Press, helping to create

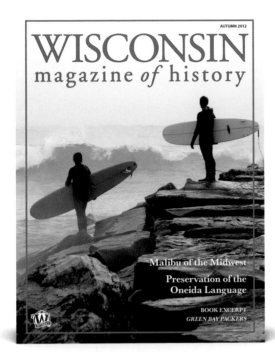

AUTUMN 2012

WISCONSIN
magazine *of* history

Malibu of the Midwest

**Preservation of the
Oneida Language**

BOOK EXCERPT
GREEN BAY PACKERS

The award-winning
*Wisconsin Magazine
of History* publishes
well-researched,
well-written, and
lavishly illustrated
articles on a wide
variety of Wisconsin
history topics.

Wisconsin Vietnam War Stories and a number of films based on Press titles, including *Fill 'Er Up* and *Bottoms Up: A Toast to Wisconsin's Historic Bars & Breweries*, which are part of the Press's Places Along the Way series. In the future, working with these and other organizations will help the Press retain a synthesis between first-rate scholarship and popular appeal.

At the heart of the Press's recent efforts is the conviction that quality stories, well told, shared in print, have the power to move and engage readers. As an example, in the early 1990s, fewer than twenty years after the fall of Saigon, the Society launched a project to collect and publish the letters and diaries of Wisconsin Vietnam War veterans. The project ultimately resulted in the Press book *Voices from Vietnam*, edited by Michael Stevens. Veterans often found it difficult to share their stories with their loved ones, yet many answered the Society's call for materials. Among them was Donald Thies, who served in the 101st Airborne Division in 1971. In the materials Thies donated was a photograph of himself and several

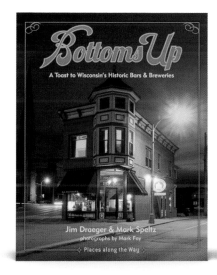
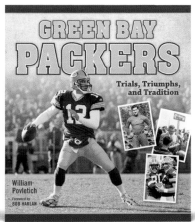

Bottoms Up: A Toast to Wisconsin's Historic Bars and Breweries, by Jim Draeger and Mark Speltz, takes readers on a tour of seventy distinctive bars and breweries around the state. *Green Bay Packers: Trials, Triumphs, and Tradition*, by William Povletich, tells the story of how one small American city came to host one of football's most iconic teams.

comrades taken just before a challenging mission that lasted several days. When the Press reprinted the title recently, this photograph was selected to be on the cover. Thies was so touched by the use of his image that he contacted all of the veterans shown in the photo and had them sign a poster-sized image of the cover. He later presented the poster to Society director Ellsworth Brown.

This new direction—publishing quality books with wider audiences in mind—will help the Press engage new readers who do not realize they enjoy history. Through the Press's diverse catalog, readers can connect to a wide swath of past experiences, with topics ranging from sports and leisure to farming and conservation, gardening, hunting, and much more. In addition, the Press's introduction of e-books in 2010 has helped to widen its potential audience even further. Today, the Press publishes every new title both in print and electronically and has converted a large percentage of its backlist to e-book formats, as well. As of early 2014, nearly one hundred Press titles were available in both print and e-book format.

Vietnam War veteran Donald Thies presented this signed poster-sized
book cover replica to Society director Ellsworth Brown in 2012.

Though economics and technology are quickly reworking the
publishing landscape, the Press has established a successful road-
map, publishing quality books that have the power to interest,
engage, inspire, and challenge Wisconsinites of all backgrounds.

Historic Preservation

In the mid-1980s, the Wisconsin legislature gave new life to historic preservation across the state with the passage of new laws. In 1985, a new burial sites protection law strengthened the protection of burial and archaeological sites. It placed greater responsibility on state agencies to consider the impact of construction projects and land management practices on historical resources. In the past twenty-five years, the Society has expanded on these efforts to protect archaeological sites, maintaining records on burials and archaeological sites, issuing permits for investigations on public land, and administering a property tax exemptions program for owners who agree to protect important sites. In addition, educational programs raise awareness of ways that citizens can protect, enjoy, and respect local sites.

In 1987, the legislature approved a new State Register of Historic Places, a state tax credit program, and zoning and funding programs to support historic preservation. These improved programs help save irreplaceable historic resources in Wisconsin and also help promote investment within the state's borders.

To date, Wisconsin has approximately 2,300 listings on the National Register of Historic Places. These listings encompass roughly 25,000 buildings. In addition, the state is home to forty-two National Historic Landmarks, such as Taliesin and the Ringling Brothers' winter quarters in Baraboo. These listings recognize properties as varied as rural one-room schools, major university buildings, the homes of workers, and the North Woods compounds of industrialists.

The Society's State Historic Preservation Office has also created the Wisconsin Architecture and History Inventory to document significant properties around the state and to help Wisconsinites research their properties. The Inventory is a digital source of information on more than 133,000 historic buildings, structures, and objects throughout Wisconsin that continues to grow. Types of places listed in the inventory include round barns, log houses, metal truss bridges, small-town commercial buildings, and Queen Anne houses that reflect Wisconsin's distinct cultural landscape.

The key to the renovation of the Stoughton Opera House was a spirit of civic volunteerism, a phased restoration plan, and persistent fund-raising efforts. The refurbished theater was rededicated on February 22, 2001, on the one-hundredth anniversary of its original opening.

Each property has a digital record providing basic information about the site, and most include exterior images. More than two hundred thousand images of these properties are available online.

The Society has worked with Wisconsin businesses and home-owners to ensure they qualify for federal and state tax credits to help preserve their properties. As a result, nearly $1 billion has been invested in Wisconsin since the mid-1970s for work to preserve the state's built heritage. Since 1976, the Society has certified nearly 500 projects that helped preserve income-producing buildings, which in turn brought $150 million in federal tax credits back to the state. A similar program for homeowners since 1992 has resulted in 2,166 projects with a total investment of more than $100 million. Through the program, abandoned warehouses and schools have been turned into desirable apartments, and empty downtown storefronts now house restaurants and shops, adding a renewed vibrancy to Wisconsin cities and towns.

As a state abutted by two of the Great Lakes, with thousands of smaller lakes within its borders, not all of Wisconsin's archaeological sites are on land. The Society administers a nationally recognized underwater archaeology program. Wisconsin waters hold a wide variety of objects to be explored, documented, and preserved, from thousand-year-old dugout canoes to nineteenth- and twentieth-century shipwrecks. Naturally, since Wisconsin waters have witnessed seven hundred shipwrecks, downed vessels comprise many underwater archaeological sites. But several hundred other prehistoric and historic sites are known to exist on the beds of Wisconsin's lakes and rivers. The Society's underwater

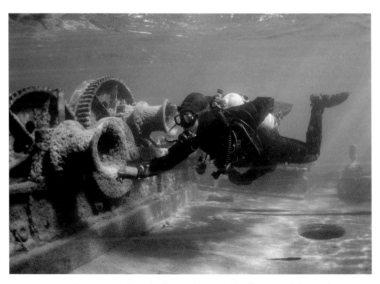

An underwater archaeologist explores a Lake Superior shipwreck.

archaeology program has investigated nearly eighty archaeological sites throughout the state. As a result of these efforts, seventeen Wisconsin shipwrecks have been placed on the National Register of Historic Places. With 860 miles of Great Lakes shoreline, 14,000 inland lakes, and thousands of miles of rivers and streams, the underwater archaeology program has a wide-ranging responsibility for studying and protecting all of the underwater archaeological resources that lie beneath the state's waters.

The Society's historic preservation efforts have had visible and lasting effects across Wisconsin. From a Finnish farmstead in Oulu to the Jeffris Flats apartments in Janesville, the Society has aided the renovation and revitalization of buildings and neighborhoods across the state. One recent example is the renovation of the historic Pabst Brewery complex, assisted by the State Historic Preservation Office through federal income tax credits. The first building to be completed on the twenty-one-acre Pabst Brewery site is the Blue Ribbon Loft Apartments, a three-story, 140,000-square-foot brick building originally called the Washhouse and Cooper Shop. This building was converted into a ninety-five-unit live/work loft-style rental apartment community. During construction, the developer reserved a percentage of the jobs to train unskilled workers from the surrounding neighborhood in the construction trades. This development has revived one of Milwaukee's most iconic buildings while supporting new businesses, providing affordable housing, and allowing residents to live and work downtown. Additionally, the project is an important catalyst for the future development of the historically significant Pabst Brewery site and has brought federal dollars to Wisconsin. Through efforts like the Pabst Brewery renovation, the Society preserves significant structures while also stimulating job creation, investment, and economic growth around the state.

THE WISCONSIN HISTORICAL FOUNDATION

The Wisconsin Historical Society is unusual in that it is both a membership organization and a state agency. In 1853, the Society received its charter from the legislature as a private corporation with a public purpose, and it received funding from the state for the first time in 1854. In 1949, the state recognized that the Society "had become a state agency through increased legislative control over [its] activities."[14] For example, the Society had been depositing its funds in the state treasury since 1920, its employees were subject to civil service regulations, its operations and funding were largely controlled by state statute, and the Society held all property as trustee for the state.[15]

The Society has always had to supplement the funds it receives from the state with other sources. These include membership dues, admission charges at historic sites, and sales of books and copies of documents and photos. In addition, volunteers have become an invaluable Society resource. In 2010, sixty-four percent of the Society's budget was covered by state tax revenue, including funding for 106.5 full-time positions.[16] That same year, volunteers provided approximately 250,000 hours of value-added labor.[17]

The Society has cultivated the support of private philanthropy for more than 150 years. While every director since Lyman Draper has actively sought private donations to increase the Society's activities and reach, an important development toward this end came in 1954 with the creation of the Wisconsin Historical Foundation.

A group of Society supporters established the Wisconsin Historical Foundation in 1954 as a nonprofit organization designed to raise private funds to help cover Society expenses. While the state has provided generous financial support to the Society since 1854, growing budgetary demands on the state steadily increased the need for private funding sources as the twentieth century came to a close.[18] Recognizing the need for more vigorous fundraising, the Wisconsin Historical Foundation hired its first paid employee in 1998. The staff has since grown to fifteen, and the Foundation performs four distinct functions for the Society: financial stewardship, administering the Society's membership program, securing major gifts to the Society, and seeking strategic financial support for Society initiatives.

In 2006, the Foundation embarked on its first major philanthropic effort, *Forward! The Campaign for the Wisconsin Historical*

Society. While the *Forward!* Campaign set a goal of raising seventy-seven million dollars, the campaign was also envisioned as a movement to engage a broad coalition of people in using history to understand their own stories and to pass these stories on to the next generation. To accomplish this, the *Forward!* Campaign set four goals: transform the historic sites to provide engaging and educational experiences that are authentic, varied, and unique; update the Society's digital collections and services, including modernizing the Society's website; preserve the Society's world-class collections by securing renovations to the Society's headquarters building, as well as the construction of a new storage and preservation facility to store collections and master evolving conservation techniques; and create a far-reaching community of members, donors, advocates, volunteers, and leaders to take a more active role in discovering and appreciating their history.

The effects of the *Forward!* Campaign are visible throughout the state. They offer a compelling vision of the superb things that can be accomplished through the combined efforts of involved citizens and state support. In April 2010, the Society celebrated a $2.9 million restoration of the Library reading room. During the seven-month project, the room regained its original magnificence. Craftspeople carefully replaced fluorescent lights with a reconstructed stained glass skylight, added new furnishings, lighting, and shelving, and restored many of the historic details that had been obscured or gone missing in a 1955 renovation. The restoration was celebrated as one of the biggest successes of the *Forward!* Campaign then to date.[19]

On November 8, 2011, the Society broke ground for a visitor center and new home for the Wesley W. Jung Carriage Museum on the grounds of the historic Wade House in Greenbush. The new facilities opened to the public on June 8, 2013, sixty years to the week after the opening of Wade House. The 38,000-square-foot, $13.5 million building overlooks bustling Highway 23, midway between Sheboygan and Fond du Lac. It offers a year-round, state-of-the-art facility showcasing Wade House's outstanding collections and serving as a powerful tool for education and service to the community. Notably, the project received about fifty-five percent of its funding from the state; the remaining forty-five percent was paid by private donations. The *Forward!* Campaign was also instrumental in funding a new 3,060-square-foot multipurpose facility at Old World Wisconsin that houses a number of functions from curatorial and administrative staff spaces to training areas for costumed interpreters.[20]

Today, the Society finds itself in much the same place as Richard Magoon and Chauncey Britt in 1845: documenting history, even as it happens. Increasing support for the Society will be crucial in ensuring that this age is remembered not merely as a bright period in the Society's long history but also as the foundation for a Society of enduring stability, strength, and scope. While so much has been accomplished, the Society has high aspirations for the future, as it embraces new technologies, safeguards its world-class collections, transforms its historic sites, and, perhaps most importantly, seeks to engage the broadest possible public audience.

Conclusion

A SOLEMN TRUST

As a former director of the Wisconsin Historical Society once noted, "The varied programs of the Society make it a state version of the Library of Congress, the National Archives, and the Smithsonian Institution, all rolled into one."[1]

The Society has grown from a small gathering of pioneers in 1846 into a multifaceted organization with twelve thousand members from every state and several countries. Yet the basic mission of the Society has remained largely unchanged: to collect, preserve, and share Wisconsin's stories.

The Wisconsin Historical Society has long been a leader among the United States' historical societies. Unlike historical societies on the eastern seaboard that had restrictive memberships, the Society has been open to anyone willing to pay dues since its beginning in 1846. At a time when history was largely the tale of past politics and battlefield glory, the Society documented the lives of rich and poor, famous and unknown. Collecting contemporary history has been a constant focus, whether it was Lyman Draper collecting the papers of land speculator Daniel Boone or modern-day archivists collecting websites of contemporary politics. The Society's collections contain information on the lives of groups who have been traditionally ignored, such as women and people of color. The Society also long served as an innovative model for other states, which have developed programs that were first tried in Wisconsin.

While commonalities over time abound, the Society has remained responsive to changing circumstances. Lyman Draper built a world-class Library and manuscript collection without the help of a wealthy benefactor; instead, he secured regular state funding, making the Wisconsin Historical Society the oldest publicly funded historical society in the United States. Reuben Gold

Thwaites transformed the Society into an engine of public education, leading the way for similar changes in historical societies around the nation. Clifford Lord helped the Society evolve from a scholarly research institution into a public service institution, aiming to be of use to as many people, in as many ways, as possible. Under subsequent leaders, the Society has employed the latest technologies—radio, television, and the Internet—to connect to a broader public and reach out to young and old alike to share in Wisconsin's past.

Today, the Wisconsin Historical Society is one of the most active and varied historical societies in the nation. It faces new challenges, as it has in every generation since 1846. Time, technologies, social trends, and heightened expectations transform how the Society collects, preserves, and shares our common history. It represents a covenant between generations. Just as those earlier pioneers worked to share the record of their successes and failures with subsequent generations, so the Society of today ensures that generations yet unborn will know the events of our own time. It is a solemn trust, and one that the Society has honored since 1846.

ACKNOWLEDGMENTS

This little book began as the feature article for the 2013–2014 edition of the *State of Wisconsin Blue Book*, published by the Wisconsin Legislative Reference Bureau. Although substantially revised for this printing, the work of three co-contributors named in the *Blue Book* article were instrumental in making this book possible.

Michael Edmonds's history of the Wisconsin Historical Society Library and Archives, originally published as the introduction for *A Wisconsin Fifteen* (Madison: State Historical Society of Wisconsin, 1998), formed the basis for telling the story of this division and its array of responsibilities. Helmut Knies contributed an unpublished paper that clarifies several archives functions and demonstrates how Clifford Lord and his colleagues made the Society relevant in the atomic age. Michael Stevens, longtime State Historian and administrator of the Society's Division of Historic Preservation and Public History, wrote significant portions of the text dealing with the state's historic preservation efforts and also wrote the conclusion to this book.

It is only right to acknowledge former Society director Clifford Lord as well. In addition to leading the post-Depression rebirth of the Society, Mr. Lord wrote a lengthy and wide-ranging history of the Society titled *Clio's Servant* (Madison: State Historical Society of Wisconsin, 1967). Readers interested in a more in-depth study of the Society's first one hundred years are encouraged to find a copy of Lord's book from their local library. I only regret there was no logical place in the present book to include an excerpt of Lord's elegy to the American doughnut (*Wisconsin Magazine of History* 37, no. 1 [Autumn, 1953], page 10)!

LIST OF SOCIETY DIRECTORS

Official titled indicated in parenthesis

Increase Lapham (Secretary)	1846-1854
Lyman C. Draper (Secretary)	1854–1886
Reuben G. Thwaites (Superintendent)	1884–1913
Milo M. Quaife (Superintendent)	1914–1920
Joseph Schafer (Superintendent)	1920–1941
Annie Nunns (Acting Superintendent)	*January–September* 1941
Edward P. Alexander (Superintendent)	1941–1946
Clifford L. Lord (Director)	1946–1958
Donald R. McNeil (Acting Director)	1958–1959
Leslie H. Fishel, Jr. (Director)	1959–1969
Richard A. Erney (Acting Director)	1969–1970
James Morton Smith (Director)	1970–1976
Richard A. Erney (Acting Director)	1976–1977
Richard A. Erney (Director)	1977–1985
Robert B. Thomasgard Jr. (Acting Director)	*April–September* 1985
H. Nicholas Muller III (Director)	1985–1996
Robert B. Thomasgard Jr. (Acting Director)	*April–September* 1996
George L. Vogt (Director)	1996–2002
Robert B. Thomasgard Jr. (Director)	2002–2004
Ellsworth H. Brown (Director)	2004–present

LIST OF IMAGES

Introduction

Page 2 Eben Peck cabin, WHi Image ID 2859, WHS Museum #1942.219

Chapter 1

Page 4 Solomon Juneau, WHi Image ID 2733, WHS Museum #1942.473; Byron Kilbourn, WHi Image ID 27655; Sam Marshall, WHi Image ID 1835; James Duane Doty, WHi Image ID 10020; **Page 5** Increase Lapham, WHi Image ID 1944; **Page 7** Lyman Draper, WHi Image ID 2629, Museum #1942.28; **Page 12** State Capitol drawing, WHi Image ID 3965; **Page 13** Company G roster, WHi Image ID 28378; **Page 15** Daniel S. Durrie, WHi Image ID 23291; **Page 16** library stacks, WHi Image ID 23287; **Page 17** small bookcase, WHi Image ID 97914, WHS Museum #1996.113.1 a-b; **Page 18** Reuben Gold Thwaites, WHi Image ID 62768

Chapter 2

Page 21 Thwaites in his office, WHi Image ID 38028; **Page 23** Frederick Jackson Turner's seminar, WHi Image ID 1910; **Page 25** Annie Nunns, WHi Image ID 97811; Emma Hawley, WHi Image ID 23318; **Page 27** New building under construction, WHi Image ID 35697; **Page 28** American Library Association group, WHi Image ID 45544; **Page 29** original elevator, WHi Image ID 40090; **Page 30** original reading room, WHi Image ID 74250; **Page 31** Anubis the Cat, WHi Image ID 85134; **Page 33** Charles E. Brown, WHi Image ID 80962; **Page 34** Traditional Ho-Chunk dress, WHi Image ID 61591

Chapter 3

Page 39 Milo Quaife, WHi Image ID 98885; **Page 41** First WHS Magazine issue, WHi Image ID 98888; **Page 44** American Indian burial mounds, Wisconsin Department of Natural Resources; **Page 45** Mrs. Fairchild, WHi Image ID 47621; Mrs. Fairchild's dress, WHi Image ID 47921, WHS Museum #1845.960 A-B; **Page 46** Louise Phelps Kellogg, WHi Image ID 15343; **Page 47** Robert La Follette Sr. and Jr., WHi Image ID 28147; **Page 53** Microfilm user, WHi Image ID 45989

Chapter 4

Page 55 Clifford Lord, WHi Image ID 98886; **Page 57** historical marker, Wisconsin Historical Society; **Page 58** McCormick poster, WHi Image ID 3600; **Page 60** Junior Historians, WHi Image ID 95986; **Page 62** Historymobile, WHi Image ID 98839; **Page 64** Austin Quinney, WHi Image ID 1923, WHS Museum #1942.478; Garters WHS Museum #1954.2052 a; **Page 66** Battle of Bad Axe, WHi Image ID 4522; **Page 67** Villa Louis porch, WHi Image ID 60079; Villa Louis interior, WHi Image ID 42006; **Page 68** Wade House, Wisconsin Historical Society; **Page 69** Stonefield blacksmith, Wisconsin Historical Society

Chapter 5

Page 73 WHA-TV, WHi Image ID 98936; **Page 74** Woman opposing segregation, WHi Image ID 4993; **Page 75** *Risking Everything*, WHi Image ID 97866; **Page 77** Map of ARCs, Wisconsin Historical Society, Betsy Finlay; **Page 81** Circus World wagon, Wisconsin Historical Society, CWi 2989; **Page 82** Circus World poster, Circus World Museum, CWi 18267; **Page 83** La Pointe painting, WHi Image ID 42457, MI# 1983.237.201; **Page 84** Madeline Island interpreter, Wisconsin Historical Society; Ojibwe clan petition, WHi Image ID 1871; **Page 86** Pendarvis House, Wisconsin Historical Society; **Page 88** oxen, Wisconsin Historical Society; Kruza house, Wisconsin Historical Society; **Page 90** Les Fishel, WHi Image ID 79582; **Page 91** Society under construction, WHi Image ID 98620; **Page 92** pharmacy display, WHi Image ID 27810

Chapter 6

Page 96 New Reading Room, Photo courtesy Zane Williams; **Page 97** Harry Miller, Wisconsin Historical Society, photo by Robert Granflaten; **Page 99** Necktie quilt, WHS Museum #1996.118.16, photo by Joseph Kapler; Braves jersey, WHS Museum #2006.68.1, photo by Joel Heiman; Pink flamingo, WHS Museum #1979.302 a-c, photo by Joel Heiman; **Page 101** Bennett's son, Image ID WHi 2101; **Page 102** Reed School, Wisconsin Historical Society; **Page 103** Black Point Estate, Wisconsin Historical Society; **Page 104** Carriage Classic, Wisconsin Historical Society; **Page 105** Vintage base ball, Wisconsin Historical Society; **Page 106** Joe Kapler, WHS Museum #1957.1122, photo by Joel Heiman; **Page 107** heirloom plants, Photo courtesy Nancy L. Klemp; **Page 109** Textbook cover, English, and Textbook cover, Spanish, Wisconsin Historical Society Press; School district map, Wisconsin Historical Society, Betsy Finlay; **Page 110** History Day participants, Wisconsin Historical Society; **Page 112** WHS Magazine cover, Wisconsin Historical Society; **Page 113** *Bottoms Up* cover, Wisconsin Historical Society Press; *Green Bay Packers* cover, Wisconsin Historical Society Press; **Page 114** Vietnam veteran poster, Wisconsin Historical

Society Press; **Page 116** Stoughton Opera House renovation, Wisconsin Historical Society; **Page 117** Lake Superior shipwreck, Wisconsin Historical Society, photo by Tamara Thomsen

Chapter 7

Page 124 WHS headquarters, Wisconsin Historical Society, photo by Robert Granflaten

Notes

Introduction

1. Mineral Point *Democrat*, October 22, 1845.
2. Ibid.
3. Ibid.

Chapter One

1. *Report and Collections of the State Historical Society of Wisconsin*, vol. 1 (Madison: State Historical Society of Wisconsin, 1903 [reprint]), xxxvi.
2. Ibid.
3. William Hesseltine, *Pioneer's Mission: The Story of Lyman Copeland Draper* (Madison: State Historical Society of Wisconsin, 1954), 104–105.
4. Ibid., 8.
5. Ibid.
6. Ibid., 4.
7. Ibid., 5–7, 41–42.
8. Ibid., 41.
9. Ibid., 42.
10. Ibid., 9–10.
11. Ibid.
12. Ibid., 41.
13. Ibid., 90.
14. Ibid., 96.
15. Ibid., 103, 106.
16. Increase Lapham, et al., *Addresses of Hon. I. A. Lapham, LL.D., and Hon. Edward Salomon at the dedication of the rooms in the south wing of the Capitol for the State Historical Society of Wisconsin, Wednesday evening, January 24, 1866, published by vote of the Legislature* (Madison: W. J. Park, state printer, 1866), appendix 1, 22.
17. Ibid.
18. Hesseltine, 111.
19. Ibid., 117–118.
20. *Collections*, vol. 1, xlix.
21. Ibid.
22. Ibid.

23. Michael Edmonds, "Introduction: 150 Years of the State Historical Society Library," in *A Wisconsin Fifteen*, ed. J. Kevin Graffagnino (Madison: State Historical Society of Wisconsin, 1998), 4.

24. Ibid., 5.

25. *Collections*, vol. 1, 146.

26. Ibid.

27. Clifford L. Lord, *Clio's Servant: The State Historical Society of Wisconsin, 1846–1854* (Madison: State Historical Society of Wisconsin, 1967), 45.

28. Ibid.

29. Edmonds, 5.

30. Edmonds, 5; Leslie H. Fishel Jr., "The Other Builder: Daniel S. Durrie and the State Historical Society of Wisconsin," *Wisconsin Magazine of History* 78, no. 4 (Summer 1995): 243.

31. Edmonds, 5.

32. Edward P. Alexander, "History Museums: From Curio Cabinets to Cultural Centers," *Wisconsin Magazine of History* 43, no. 3 (Spring 1960): 177.

33. Lord, *Clio's Servant*, 59, 63.

34. Alexander, 177.

35. Frederick Jackson Turner, *Reuben Gold Thwaites: A Memorial Address* (Madison: State Historical Society of Wisconsin, 1914), 15–16.

36. Hesseltine, 298.

Chapter Two

1. Hesseltine, 300.

2. *Proceedings of the Annual Meeting of the State Historical Society of Wisconsin* (Madison, State Historical Society of Wisconsin, 1889), 25–26.

3. *Proceedings*, 1892, 43.

4. Ibid., 22.

5. Ibid.

6. Reuben Gold Thwaites, "State-Supported Historical Societies and their Functions," *Annual Report of the American Historical Association*, 1897, 66.

7. Ibid., 69.

8. Ibid.

9. Ibid.

10. Frederick Jackson Turner, *Reuben Gold Thwaites: A Memorial Address* (Madison: State Historical Society of Wisconsin, 1914), 24–25.

11. *Proceedings*, 1892, 65.

12. Ibid.

13. Ibid., 66.

14. Michael Edmonds, "Introduction: 150 Years of the State Historical Society Library," in *A Wisconsin Fifteen*, ed. J. Kevin Graffagnino (Madison: State Historical Society of Wisconsin, 1998), 18.

15. "Proceedings," *Wisconsin Magazine of History* 57, no. 1 (December 1943): 69.

16. Ibid.

17. Ibid.

18. *Proceedings*, 1892, 72.

19. Ibid.

20. Reuben Gold Thwaites, "A Description of the Building," *Wisconsin State Historical Library Building Memorial Volume* (Madison: Democratic Printing Company, State Printer, 1901), 83.

21. Ibid., 89.

22. Ibid., 91.

23. Ibid., 92.

24. Ibid., 92–93.

25. Clifford L. Lord, *Clio's Servant: The State Historical Society of Wisconsin, 1846–1854* (Madison: State Historical Society of Wisconsin, 1967), 123–124.

26. Ibid.

27. "Open Bar: The Newsroom Pub," *Columbia Journalism Review*, March 1, 2013, http://www.cjr.org/currents/open_bar_ma2013.php

28. Lord, *Clio's Servant*, 125, 182.

29. Lord, *Clio's Servant*, 183–184.

30. Ibid., 184.

31. Clifford L. Lord, "Reuben Gold Thwaites," *Wisconsin Magazine of History* 47, no. 1, (Autumn 1963), 4.

32. Turner, 23.

33. "Economic History of Wisconsin during the Civil War Decade by Frederick Merk: Review by Albert H. Sanford," *The Mississippi Valley Historical Review* 4, no. 3 (December 1917): 402.

34. Lord, *Clio's Servant*, 195.

35. *Proceedings*, 1913, 29.

36. Ibid., 49–50.

37. Lord, *Clio's Servant*, 197.

38. Ibid., 196–197.

39. Ibid., 201.

Chapter Three

1. Clifford L. Lord, *Clio's Servant: The State Historical Society of Wisconsin, 1846–1854* (Madison: State Historical Society of Wisconsin, 1967), 201.

2. Ibid., 202.

3. Ibid., 228, 229–232.

4. Ibid., 229.

5. Milo Quaife, "Cannon Fodder," *Wisconsin Magazine of History* 1, no. 2 (December 1917): 192.

6. Lord, *Clio's Servant*, 257.

7. Joseph Schafer, "The Wisconsin Doomsday Book," *Wisconsin Magazine of History* 4, no. 1, (September 1920): 61.

8. Lord, *Clio's Servant*, 182–188.

9. Ibid., 318.

10. Ibid., 319.

11. "Annie Amelia Nunns, 1868–1942," *Wisconsin Magazine of History* 25, no. 3 (March 1942): 262.

Chapter Four

1. Clifford L. Lord, *Clio's Servant: The State Historical Society of Wisconsin, 1846–1854* (Madison: State Historical Society of Wisconsin, 1967), 317.

2. William A. Titus, "A Review and an Introduction," *Wisconsin Magazine of History* 25, no. 2 (December 1941): 129–130.

3. Ibid., 131.

4. Ibid.

5. Edward P. Alexander, "Wisconsin Local Historical Societies 1942–1943," *Wisconsin Magazine of History* 27, no. 4 (June 1944): 482.

6. Edward P. Alexander, "Chats with the Editor," *Wisconsin Magazine of History* 28, no. 2 (December 1944): 132.

7. Ibid.

8. Edward P. Alexander, "Chats with the Editor," *Wisconsin Magazine of History* 27, no. 2 (December 1943): 133.

9. Clifford L. Lord, "The Significance of State and Local History," *Missouri Historical Review* 44 (January 1950): 130–41.

10. Ibid., 136.

11. Clifford L. Lord, "What Are We Doing?," *Utah Historical Quarterly* 23, no. 1 (January 1955): 71.

12. Ibid.

13. Ibid., 72.

14. Ibid.

15. Lord, "The Significance of State and Local History," 139–140.

16. Sarah Davis McBride, *History Just Ahead* (Madison: Wisconsin Historical Society Press, 1999), viii.

17. Vanderbilt, Paul, "Grandma and Grandpa on the Porch," Wisconsin Magazine of History, 40:1 (autumn, 1956), 452. http://velphillips foundation.com/vel.htm [Accessed 9/15/2014]

18. "Children Make History," by Doris Platt, *Wisconsin Magazine of History* 42, no. 1 (Autumn 1958): 37.

19. Lord, *Clio's Servant*, 549, n.9.

20. Ibid., 406.

21. Ibid.

22. Ibid.

23. Doris Platt, "Children Make History: The Wisconsin Junior Historian Program," *Wisconsin Magazine of History* 42, no. 1 (Autumn 1958): 35.

24. "Our Wisconsin Letter," *Badger History* 1, no. 1 (October 1947): 2.

25. Clifford L. Lord, "Chats with the Editor," *Wisconsin Magazine of History* 31, no. 2 (December 1947): 134.

26. Lord, *Clio's Servant*, 406.

27. Clifford L. Lord, "Chats with the Editor," *Wisconsin Magazine of History* 31, no. 4 (June 1948): 389.

28. "Our Wisconsin Letter," *Badger History* 1, no. 3 (December 1947): 1.

29. "Our Wisconsin Letter," *Badger History* 1, no. 4 (January 1948): 3.

30. "Chats with the Editor," *Wisconsin Magazine of History* 31, no. 4, June 1948, 389.

31. Platt, 35.

32. "Proceedings," Autumn 1960, 56.

33. Platt, 36.

34. Ibid.

35. Ibid.

36. Ibid.

37. Ibid., 37.

38. "Proceedings," Autumn 1960, 56.

39. "Director's Report, 1977–1978," *Wisconsin Magazine of History* 61, no. 2 (Winter 1977–78): 170.

40. Clifford L. Lord, "Smoke Rings," *Wisconsin Magazine of History* 37, no. 4 (Summer 1954): 199.

41. Ibid.

42. Francis Paul Prucha, "Livia Appel and the Art of Copyediting: A Personal Memoir," *Wisconsin Magazine of History* 79, no. 4 (Summer 1996): 365n5.

43. Hass, 9.

44. Michael Edmonds, "Introduction: 150 Years of the State Historical Society Library," in *A Wisconsin Fifteen*, ed. J. Kevin Graffagnino (Madison: State Historical Society of Wisconsin, 1998), 27–28.

45. Edmonds, 29, 32.

46. Edward P. Alexander, "History Museums: From Curios Cabinets to Cultural Centers," *Wisconsin Magazine of History* 43, no. 3 (Spring 1960): 176.

47. Clifford L. Lord, "Smoke Rings," *Wisconsin Magazine of History* 39, no. 1 (Autumn 1955): 49.

48. Clifford L. Lord, "Smoke Rings," *Wisconsin Magazine of History* 42, no. 1 (Autumn 1958): 18.

Chapter Five

1. Clifford Lord, *Clio's Servant: The State Historical Society of Wisconsin, 1846–1854* (Madison: State Historical Society of Wisconsin, 1967), 295.

2. Ibid, 388.

3. Ibid., 462–463.

4. "Proceedings," *Wisconsin Magazine of History* 47, no. 1, (Autumn 1963): 67.

5. "Proceedings," *Wisconsin Magazine of History* 51, no. 1, (Autumn 1967): 78–79.

6. *Columns,* Autumn 2012, 8.

7. *Wisconsin Magazine of History* 59, no. 3 (Spring 1976): inside back cover.

8. Michael Edmonds, "Introduction: 150 Years of the State Historical Society Library," in *A Wisconsin Fifteen,* ed. J. Kevin Graffagnino (Madison: State Historical Society of Wisconsin, 1998), 36–37.

9. Ibid., 37.

10. Ibid.

11. Ibid., 37, 35.

12. "Director's Report, 1975–1976," *Wisconsin Magazine of History* 60, no. 3 (Spring 1977): 229.

13. "Director's Report, 1973–1974," *Wisconsin Magazine of History* 58, no. 1 (Autumn 1974): 74.

14. "Proceedings," *Wisconsin Magazine of History* 54, no. 1 (Autumn 1970): 70.

15. "Proceedings," *Wisconsin Magazine of History* 55, no. 1 (Autumn 1971): 67.

16. "Proceedings," Autumn 1970, 70.

17. "Proceedings," *Wisconsin Magazine of History* 57, no. 1 (Autumn 1973): 71.

18. "Proceedings," *Wisconsin Magazine of History* 64, no. 1 (Autumn 1980): 70.

19. "Director's Report, 1980–81," *Wisconsin Magazine of History* 65, no. 1 (Autumn 1981): 72.

Chapter Six

1. Edmonds., 38.

2. Ibid., 38–39.

3. Ibid., 38.

4. "Black Dahlia, French Angel, Sterling Hall Bombing," *Mysteries at the Museum,* Travel Channel, http://www.travelchannel.com/tv-shows/mysteries-at-the-museum/episodes/black-dahlia

5. Edward P. Alexander, "History Museums: From Curios Cabinets to Cultural Centers," *Wisconsin Magazine of History* 43, no. 3 (Spring 1960): 176.

6. "Report of the Supervisor: Office of School Services," Minutes of the Board of Curators [of the State Historical Society of Wisconsin], January 26, 1963, 12. Wisconsin Historical Society Archives, Series 932, Madison, Wisconsin.

7. Ibid.

8. "Director's Report," Minutes of the Board of Curators [of the State Historical Society of Wisconsin], January 30, 1965, 11. Wisconsin Historical Society Archives, Series 932, Madison, Wisconsin.

9. Ibid.

10. *National History Day in Wisconsin 2011–2012: A Year in Review,* (Madison: State Historical Society of Wisconsin, 2012), 3.

11. *2011–2012 National History Day in Wisconsin Program Statistics* (Madison: State Historical Society of Wisconsin, 2012).

12. *National History Day in Wisconsin 2011–2012: A Year in Review,* 2.

13. Ibid., 4.

14. Opinions of the Attorney General of the State of Wisconsin, 74 O.A.G., 54, 55 (1985).

15. 2009–2010 Wisconsin Statutes & Annotations 44.01(1), https://docs.legis.wisconsin.gov/statutes/statutes/44

16. "Wisconsin Historical Society Biannual Report, 2009–2011," 10, http://www.wisconsinhistory.org/about/budget/09-11-biennium/pdfs/2009-2011-SocietyBiennialReport-Final.pdf

17. Ibid., 6.

18. William Hesseltine, *Pioneer's Mission: The Story of Lyman Copeland Draper* (Madison: State Historical Society of Wisconsin, 1954), 121–123.

19. "2010 Year in Review," Wisconsin Historical Society, http://www.wisconsinhistory.org/about/budget/pdfs/2010-Year-in-Review.pdf

20. Ibid.

Conclusion

1. "Proceedings of the One Hundred and Twenty-fifth Annual Business Meeting of The State Historical Society of Wisconsin: Director's Report," by James Morton Smith, *Wisconsin Magazine of History* 55:1 (Autumn, 1971), 66.

INDEX

Page numbers in *italics* refer to images.

African Americans, 2, 93, 99, 123
  The Black Community: Its Culture and Heritage (exhibit), 93
  civil rights movement, 73–76, *74*, *75*
  Freedom Summer (exhibit), 75
  Mississippi Burning (film), 74
  necktie quilt, *99*
  Risking Everything: A Freedom Summer Reader (Edmonds), 74, 75
agriculture
  farm implement exhibits, 33, 70
  Old World Wisconsin, 81, 86–87, *88*, 91, 93, 98, 106–107, 121
  State Agricultural Museum, 70
  Stonefield, 65, 69–70, *69*
Alexander, Edward P., 49, 51–54, 72, 95, 127
  as editor, 51
  education, 51
  resignation, 54
American Association of State and Local History, 111
American Federation of Labor collection, 57
American Fur Company, 83–85, *83*
American Historical Association Public Archives Commission, 32
American Hotel, 3
American Indians. *See* Indians
American Revolution Bicentennial, 49, 89
Antiquarian Fund, 33
Antiques Road Show (television program), 106
Anubis the Cat, 31–32, *31*
Appel, Livia, 63
archaeology, 1, 33, 36, 57, 78–79, 80, 98, 115
  burial sites protection program, 80, 115

effigy mounds, 5, 11, 44, *44*, 57, 78
  Highway Archaeology Salvage Program, 80
  Museum Archaeology Program, 80
  State Archaeologist, 71
  underwater, 117–118, *117*
  Wisconsin Archaeological Society, 78
architecture, 57, 86–87
  Wisconsin Architecture and History Inventory, 115–116
Archives, 1, 9, 11, 21, 32, 47, 57, 71, 89, 92, 95–98, *97*
  American Federation of Labor collection, 57
  Area Research Center system, 76, *77*
  Cyrus Hall McCormick collection, 57, 58
  Father James Groppi collection, 75
  International Workingman's Association collection, 73
  Mass Communications History Center, 58
  McCormick-International Harvester Company collection, 57, 58, *58*
  National Broadcasting Company collection, 58
  Wisconsin Archives Act, 32, 40
Area Research Center system, 76, *77*
  map, *77*
Astor, John Jacob, 83
Aztalan, 78, 79

Badger Biographies series, 108
Badger History (magazine), 60–61, 110
Baraboo, WI
  Circus World Museum, 81
  Man Mound, *78*
  Ringling Brothers winter quarters, 115
Bates, Daisy, 74
Battle of Bad Axe (painting), *66*
Bayfield, WI, 83

Beecroft, Lillian, 49
Belmont, WI
    First Capitol, 98, 100
Bennett, Ashley, *101*
Bennett, Harry Hamilton, 100, 101, 106
Bennett (H. H.) Studio, 100, 101
Berger, Victor, 73
"Big Three," 24, 37, 41
*The Black Community: Its Culture and
    Heritage* (exhibit), 93
Black Point Estate, 103, *103*
Blue Ribbon Loft Apartments, 118
Board of Curators, 10, 41, 42, 51. *See
    also* executive committee
Boone, Daniel, 8–9, 123
    papers in Draper Manuscripts, 18
*Bottoms Up: A Toast to Wisconsin's Historic
    Bars & Breweries* (Draeger &
    Speltz), 112, *113*
Brant, Joseph
    papers in Draper Manuscripts, 18
Breakfast in a Victorian Kitchen, 104
*The British Regime in Wisconsin and the
    Northwest* (Kellogg), 48
Britt, Chauncey, 1, 3, 36, 121
broadcast media. *See* communications
    media
Brown, Charles E., 32–33, *33*, 44, 46,
    48, 49, 72, 79
Brown, Ellsworth H., 100, 113, 114, 127
Burger, Warren, 90
burial sites protection program, 80, 115

Cabinet, 7, 16, 18, 24. *See also* Museum
capitol building, *15*, 22, 26
    fire, 26, 32
    First Capitol, 98–100
    Governor's Room, 5, 6
    Library, 6, 11, *16*, *23*
    meetings, 3, 5
    territorial capitol, 3, *12*
Capser, Bella, 83
Capser, Leo, 83
Capser Center, 85
Carriage Classic, 104, *104*
Cassville, WI
    Stonefield, 69
Chaney, James, 74
Chicago and the Northwest (Quaife), 39
Cindy Bentley: Spirit of a Champion

(Special Olympics of Wisconsin),
    111
Circus World Museum, 81–83, *81, 82*
    funding, 82
    Ringling Brothers Circus Train
        complex, 82
    Ringling Brothers' winter quarters,
        81, 115
    Ringling Camel House, 82
    Ringling Ring Barn, 82
    Water for Elephants (film), 106
civil rights movement, 73–76, *74, 75*
    Freedom Summer (exhibit), 75
    Groppi, Father James, 75
    Mississippi Burning (film), 74
    *Risking Everything: A Freedom Summer
        Reader* (Edmonds), 74, 75
Civil War, 12, 34–35, 100
    Centennial, 49, 89
    The Civil War Era (History of Wiscon-
        sin series), 90
    commemorative roster, *13*
    *Doctrine of Non-Intervention with
        Slavery in the Territories* (Quaife), 39
    *The Economic History of Wisconsin
        During the Civil War Decade*
        (Merk), 35
    *Narrative of Service with the Third Wis-
        consin Infantry* (Hinkley), 35
    photographic collections, 33
    reenactments, 105
    Wisconsin Women in the War (Hurn),
        35
The Civil War Era (History of Wisconsin
    series), 90
Clark, George Rogers
    papers in Draper Manuscripts, 18
Collections (Wisconsin Historical Soci-
    ety), 13–14, 33–34, 40, 45–46
communications media, 72
    Mass Communications History
        Center, 58
    National Broadcasting Company
        collection, 58
    radio, 44, 72–73, 95, 124
    television, 59, 72–73, *73*, 95, 106, 124
    Wisconsin Center for Film and The-
        ater Research, 58–59
computers, 34, 89, 95–98, 113, 116,
    120, 124

Congress of Racial Equality, 73
Continuity and Change (History of Wisconsin series), 90
Courier (newspaper), 3
Creating Dairyland (Wisconsin Milk Marketing Board), 111

Democrat (newspaper), 1
Dengel, Isabella, 2
Depression, 37, 45, 47–48, 52, 55, 63, 66
War, a New Era, and Depression (History of Wisconsin series), 90
Dewey, Nelson, 8
Stonefield, 69
WHS president, 5
Diary of James K. Polk (Quaife), 39
Dillinger (film), 106
directors, 5, 37, 127
died, 36–37, 48
elected, 5, 11, 19
hired, 37, 42, 51, 54
resigned, 42, 54, 70
retired, 21
See also Alexander, Edward P.; Brown, Ellsworth H.; Draper, Lyman Copeland; Erney, Richard A.; Fishel, Leslie H., Jr.; Lapham, Increase; Lord, Clifford L.; Muller, H. Nicholas, III; Quaife, Milo Milton; Schafer, Joseph; Smith, James Morton; Thwaites, Reuben Gold; Vogt, George L.
displays. *See* exhibits
Doctrine of Non-Intervention with Slavery in the Territories (Quaife), 39
Documentary History of the Ratification of the Constitution (National Historical Records and Publications Commission), 90–91
Doomsday Project, 43, 48
Doty, James Duane
WHS officer, 3–4, *4*
Dousman, Hercules
Villa Louis, 65–66
Dousman, Louis
Villa Louis, 65–66
Draper, Harriet, 7
Draper, Jonathan, 6
Draper, Luke, 6

Draper, Lyman Copeland, 6–19, *7*, 21, 22, 34, 35, 37, 40, 49, 51, 78, 91, 95, 98, 123, 127
as author, 7, 8–9, 12, 13, 19
birth, 6
death, 17
education, 7, 8
employment, 8
retirement, 21
Draper Manuscripts, 17–18, 46, 48
Duckett, Kenneth, *53*
Durrie, Daniel S., 15, *15*, 22

Eagle, WI
Old World Wisconsin, 87
The Economic History of Wisconsin During the Civil War Decade (Merk), 35
Edmonds, Michael
Risking Everything: A Freedom Summer Reader, 74, 75
education, *23*, 24, 36, 37, 42, 44, 45, 52, 80, 95, 115, 124
Badger Biographies series, 108
Badger History (magazine), 60–61, 110
Historymobile, 62–63, *62*
Junior Historian program, 59–60, *60*, 61–62, 108–110
map, *109*
National History Day, 95, 110–111, *110*
New Badger History series, 107–108
Reed School, 100–102, *102*
textbooks, 108, *109*
"Thinking Like a Historian" method, 108
effigy mounds, 5, 11, 44, *44*, 78
historical marker, *57*
Man Mound, 78
panther intaglio, 57
employees. *See* staff
Erney, Richard A., 93, 127
ethnology, 33, 57, 98
executive committee, 5, 9, 10, 13, 32, 47. *See also* Board of Curators
exhibits, 9, 24, 30, 36, 44, 45, *45*, 52–53, *64*, 71, 92–93
Anubis the Cat, 31–32, *31*
The Black Community: Its Culture and Heritage, 93

Civil War commemorative roster, *13*
farm implements, 33, 70
firefighting, 33
Freedom Summer, 75
Frontier Wisconsin, 93
History through Our Historic Sites, 62
Historymobile, 62–63, *62*
The Immigrant State, 93
lumbering, 33
Madeline Island Museum, 85
Making a Living, 93
Milwaukee Braves' uniform, *99*
necktie quilt, *99*
Ojibwe petition, *84*
People of the Woodlands, 93
pharmacy display, 92–93, *92*
philatelic display, 45
Philip La Follette, 93
pink flamingo, *99*
The Political Arena, 93
post office, 33
Sawdust and Spangles: The Circus in Wisconsin, 62
Sense of Community, 93
Signers of the Declaration of Independence, 62
Wisconsin: Wilderness, Territory, Frontier, 62
Wisconsin women, 93

Fairchild, Frances, *45*
Fairchild, Lucius, 45
farm museums. *See* agriculture
Farwell, Leonard
WHS president, 9
Fill 'Er Up (Draeger & Speltz), 112
films and documentaries
Dillinger (film), 106
Mississippi Burning (film), 74
The Presence of Our Past (film), 72
Water for Elephants (film), 106
Wisconsin Center for Film and Theater Research, 58–59
First Annual Report and Collections of the State Historical Society of Wisconsin (WHS), 13–14
First Baptist Church, 11
First Capitol, 98–100
Council House, 100
lodging house, 100

Fish, Carl Russell, 40
Fishel, Leslie H., Jr., 71, 73, 87, *90*, 127
Fond du Lac, WI
historic preservation ordinance, 80
Fort Atkinson, WI
historical marker, *57*
Fort Winnebago, 78
Forward! The Campaign for the Wisconsin Historical Society, 119–121
Foster, Mary Stuart, 24, 49
founders
Britt, Chauncey, 1, 3, 36, 121
Magoon, Richard, 1, 121
Fox, Thurman, *60*
Freedom Summer (exhibit), 75
From Exploration to Statehood (History of Wisconsin series), *90*
Frontier Wisconsin (exhibit), 93
fur trade, 21, 83–85, *83, 84*

genealogy, 15, 30, 89
Goodland, Walter, 56
Goodman, Andrew, 74
government documents, 5, 11, 14, 28, 32, 39–40, 76, 97
Journals (Wisconsin Territory), 5
Laws (Wisconsin Territory), 5
Wisconsin Archives Act, 32, 40
government funding, 2, 10, 22–23, 27, 32, 35, 43, 45, 47, 79, 106, 119, 121, 123
Grandma's Attic (television program), 72
Great Depression, 37, 45, 47–48, 52, 55, 63, 66
War, a New Era, and Depression (History of Wisconsin series), *90*
Green Bay, WI
Hazelwood, 78
historical marker, 57
local historical society, 25
Green Bay Packers: Trials, Triumphs, and Tradition (Povletich), *113*
Greenbush, WI
Wade House, 66, *68*, 120
Groppi, Father James, 75

Hamlin, Amos C., Jr., 64
Haskell, Frank, 35
Hawley, Emma, 25, *25*

Hazelwood, 78
headquarters, 14, 26–32, *27, 28, 29, 30,*
    35, 36, 46–47, 63, 71, 91–93, *91,*
    96, 120, *124*
  capitol building, 5–6, *15,* 16, 22, 23,
    26
  First Baptist Church, 11
  territorial capitol, 3, *12*
Hearthside Dinner, 105
Hellum, Edgar, 85–86
Herrling Sawmill, 68
Hesseltine, William, 63
Highway Archaeology Salvage Program,
    80
historic preservation, 1, 76–81,
    115–118. *See also* archaeology;
    Historic Sites
  Aztalan, 78, 79
  Blue Ribbon Loft Apartments, 118
  Fort Winnebago, 78
  Hazelwood, 78
  Historic Preservation Division, 80
  Integrated Park Act, 78
  Jeffris Flats apartments, 118
  La Farge Reservoir Project, 80
  Little White Schoolhouse, 78
  local efforts, 80–81
  Millville, WI, 79
  National Historic Landmarks, 115
  National Historic Preservation Act,
    79, 80
  National Register of Historic Places,
    79, 115, 118
  Old Agency House, 78
  Pabst Brewery, 118
  Saint Augustine Church, 78
  shipwrecks, 117–118, *117*
  State Historic Preservation Office,
    79, 80, 115, 118
  State Register of Historic Places, 79,
    115
  Stoughton Opera House, *116*
  tax credit programs, 80, 115, 116–117,
    118
  Wisconsin Architecture and History
    Inventory, 115–116
Historic Sites, 1, 71, 81–88, 100–107,
    120, 121
  Bennett (H. H.) Studio, 100, 101
  Black Point Estate, 103, *103*

Circus World Museum, 81–83, *81,*
    82, 106
  events, 104–105, *104, 105*
  First Capitol, 98–100
  History through Our Historic Sites
    (exhibit), 62
  Madeline Island Museum, 81,
    83–85, *84,* 102
  map, *77*
  Old World Wisconsin, 81, 86–87, *88,*
    91, 93, 98, *105,* 106–107, *107,* 121
  Pendarvis, 81, 85–86, *86*
  Reed School, 100–102, *102*
  Stonefield, 65, 69–70, *69*
  Villa Louis, 65–66, *67,* 104, *104*
  Wade House, 66–68, *68,* 105,
    120–121
  Wisconsin Historical Sites and Mark-
    ers Committee, 57
historical markers, 25, 56–57, *57*
  Wisconsin Historical Sites and Mark-
    ers Committee, 57
Historical Society of Wisconsin, 10. *See*
    also Wisconsin Historical Society
History of Wisconsin series (WHS Press),
    90
History Sandwiched In program, 105
History through Our Historic Sites (ex-
    hibit), 62
Historymobile, 62–63, *62*

The Immigrant State (exhibit), 93
Indians, 2, 4, 11, 12, 14, 21, 33, *34, 64,*
    76, 85
  archaeology, 5, 11, 44, *44,* 78, 79, 98
  A Nation within a Nation: Voices of
    the Oneidas in Wisconsin (Oneida
    Tribe of Indians), 111
  Ojibwe petition, *84*
  People of the Woodlands (exhibit), 93
  Perkins Collection, 18
  Quinney, Austin E., *64*
Integrated Park Act, 78
International Workingman's Associa-
    tion collection, 73

Jaggi, Casper (Badger Biography), 108
Janesville, WI
  Jeffris Flats apartments, 118
Jeffris Flats apartments, 118

Jesuit Relations (Thwaites), 33
Journals (Wisconsin Territory), 5
Journals of Lewis and Clark (Thwaites), 33
Juneau, Solomon
  WHS officer, 3, *4*
Junior Historian program, 59–60, *60*, 61–62, 108–110

Kapler, Joe, *106*
Kellogg, Louise Phelps, 40, 45–46, *46*, 48, 49, 72
  The British Regime in Wisconsin and the Northwest, 48
Kent, Alan E., *53*
Kenton, Simon
  papers in Draper Manuscripts, 18
Kilbourn, Byron
  WHS officer, 3, *4*
Kohler, Marie, 68
Kohler, Ruth DeYoung, 68
Kruza house, *88*

labor unions. *See* organized labor
La Farge Reservoir Project, 80
La Follette, Philip, 93
La Follette, Robert, Jr., *47*
La Follette, Robert, Sr., *47*
Lake Geneva, WI
  Black Point Estate, 103, *103*
Lake Mills, WI
  Aztalan, 79
Lambeau, Curly (Badger Biography), 108
Lapham, Increase
  WHS officer, 3, 5, *5*, 78, 127
La Pointe, WI
  Madeline Island Museum, *83*, 85
Larrabee, Charles, 8, 9, 10
Laws (Wisconsin Territory), 5
Leadership in History Awards, 111
Library, 1, 9, 11, 14, 15, *16*, *17*, *23*, 24, 46, 48, 52, 123
  book sales, 33
  cataloging, 22, 28, 36, 95–96
  classification, 22, 89
  collections, 5, 11, 14, 16–17, 21–22, 26, 28, 36, 37, 42, 52, 89, 95
  genealogy, 15, 30, 89

government documents, 5, 11, 14, 28, 32, 39–40, 76, 97
  interlibrary loan, 42
  location, 6, 11, 16, *17*, 27–29, 31, 35, 46–47, 63
  reading room, 27, 28–29, *30*, *96*, 120
  research, 22, 28, 34, 36, 63, 89
  space problems, 11, 16, *17*, 35, 46–47, 52, 63, 91
  staff, 15, *15*, 22, 24, *25*, 45–46, *46*, 49, 72, 74, 89
  statistics, 6, 11, 16, 18, 29, 31, 35
  technology, 18, 28, 34, 48, 52, *53*, 89, 95–98, 113
  users, 1, 23, *23*, 37, 55, 89, 96, 124
Little White Schoolhouse, 78
local historical societies, 1, 25–26, 34, 43, 51–52, 56–57, 107
  Green Bay, WI, 25
  Ripon, WI, 25
  Sauk County, WI, 78
Logmark Editions, 63
Lord, Charles, 9
Lord, Clifford L., 49, 54–59, *55*, *60*, 61, 63, 70, 71, 95, 124, 127
  resignation, 70
Lori's Log Cabin (television program), 72

MacQuarrie, Ellen, *31*
Madeline Island Museum, 81, 83–85, *84*
  American Fur Company, 83–85, *83*
  Capser Center, 85
  funding, 85, 102
  La Pointe jail, 85
  Old Sailor's Home, 85
  Walkway Gallery, 85
Madison, WI, 3, 8, 98
  first building, *2*
  historic preservation ordinance, 80
  Madison Park and Pleasure Drive Association, 44
  WHA (radio), 72
  WHA-TV (television), 72, *73*
  Wisconsin State Journal (newspaper), 18, 19
Madison Park and Pleasure Drive Association, 44
Magoon, Richard, 1, 121

Mai Ya's Long Journey (Badger Biography series), 108
Making a Living (exhibit), 93
Maps
  Area Research Center system, *77*
  Historic Sites, *77*
  school districts, *109*
Marshall, Samuel
  WHS officer, 3, *4*
Mass Communications History Center, 58
"Matriarchy," 24, 41
McCormick, Cyrus Hall, 57, 58
McCormick-International Harvester Company collection, 57, 58, *58*
McNeil, Donald R., 127
Memoirs of Jeremiah Curtin (Schafer), 48
Merk, Frederick, 35
Merry Christmas Mine, 86
Metropolitan Baptist Church, 99
microfilm, 18, 48, 52, *53*
Miller, Harry, *97*
Millville, WI, 79
Milwaukee, WI
  civil rights movement, 74, 75
  Courier (newspaper), 3
  historic preservation ordinance, 80
  Pabst Brewery complex, 118
Milwaukee Press Club, 31–32
Milwaukee Public Schools, 108
Mineral Point, WI
  Democrat (newspaper), 1
  historic preservation ordinance, 80
  Pendarvis, 85–86, *86*
  mining, 85–86
Minocqua, WI, 108
Mississippi Burning (film), 74
Mississippi Freedom Summer, 74–75, *75*
Monroe, WI, 108
Moore, Amzie, 74
Morrison's American Hotel, 3
MTM Enterprises collection, 59
Muller, H. Nicholas, III, 98, 127
Museum, 1, 7, 16, 24, 30–31, 32–33, 35–36, 37, 43–45, 48, 63, 79, 91–93, 98
  Antiques Road Show (television program), 106
  exhibits, 9, 24, 33, 36, 44, 45, *45*,
52–53, 62–63, *64*, 71, 92–93, *92*, *99*
  films and documentaries, 106
  History Sandwiched In program, 105
  Historymobile, 62–63, *62*
  inventory, 93
  Museum Archaeology Program, 80
  Mysteries at the Museum (television program), 106
  Perkins Collection, 18
  philatelic collection, 45
  relocation, 93
  space, 52, 63, 71, 91–93
  staff, 30–31, 32–33, *33*, 44, 49, 53, 72, 79
  Taste Traditions of Wisconsin program, 105
  Van Schaick collection, 34
  visual materials collection, *2, 9, 16, 24, 30, 33, 34, 59, 64, 66, 71, 100,* 106
Museum Archaeology Program, 80
Mysteries at the Museum (television program), 106

Narrative of Service with the Third Wisconsin Infantry (Hinkley), 35
A Nation within a Nation: Voices of the Oneidas in Wisconsin (Oneida Tribe of Indians), 111
National Broadcasting Company collection, 58
National Historic Landmarks, 115
  Ringling Brothers' winter quarters, 81, 115
  Taliesin, 115
National Historic Preservation Act, 79, 80
National Historical Records and Publications Commission
  Documentary History of the Ratification of the Constitution, 90–91
National History Day, 95, 110–111, *110*
National Register of Historic Places, 79, 115, 118
Native Americans. *See* Indians
Neal, Robert, 85–86
Neillsville, WI
  Reed School, 100–102, *102*
New Badger History series, 107–108

New Diggings, WI
  Saint Augustine Church, 78
Newcomb, Kate Pelham (Badger Biography), 108
Newsroom Pub, 32
Nicolet landing (historical marker), 57
Northern Great Lakes Visitor Center, 76
Nunns, Annie, 24, *25*, 37, 41, 49, 51, 127

Office of Local History, 71
officers, *4*, 10
  elections, 3, 4, 5, 11, 19
  presidents, 5, 9, 51
  secretaries, 5, 11, 19, 78, 127
  treasurers, 5, 13
  vice presidents, 3, 5
Old Agency House, 78
Old Sailor's Home, 85
Old World Wisconsin, 81, 86–87, *88*, 91, 93, 98, 106–107, 121
  Dillinger (film), 106
  dinner theater, 105
  gardens, *107*
  Kruza house, *88*
  vintage baseball, *105*
oral history, 1, 7–8, 9–10, 21
organized labor, 2, 57–58, 73, 74
  American Federation of Labor, 57
  International Workingman's Association, 73
Oshkosh, WI, 18
  Times (newspaper), 19
Oulu, WI
  historic preservation, 118

Pabst Brewery, 118
Paul, Les (Badger Biography), 108
Peck, Eben
  cabin (painting), *2*
Pendarvis, 81, 85–86, *86*
  Merry Christmas Mine, 86
  Polperro, 86
  Shake Rag Street, 86
  Trelawny, 86
People of the Woodlands (exhibit), 93
Perkins Collection, 18
Perrin, Richard, 86
Peshtigo Fire Cemetery (historical marker), 57
Peters, Cal, 66

Phillips, Vel, 75–76
Places Along the Way series
  Bottoms Up: A Toast to Wisconsin's Historic Bars & Breweries (Draeger & Speltz), 112, *113*
  Fill 'Er Up (Draeger & Speltz), 112
"the plumber from Kenosha," 54–55
The Political Arena (exhibit), 93
Polperro, 86
Portage, WI
  Fort Winnebago, 78
  Old Agency House, 78
Potter, John, 106
Potter Knife, *106*
Prairie du Chien, WI
  Villa Louis, 66
The Presence of Our Past (film), 72
presidents (WHS), 5, 9, 51
Proceedings (Wisconsin Historical Society), 33–34, 48
The Progressive Era (History of Wisconsin series), 90
public relations, 22–23, 28, 44, 45, 55, 63, 72, 90, 95
publishing. *See* Wisconsin Historical Society Press

Quaife, Milo Milton, 37, 39–42, *39*, 51, 127
  as author, 39, 40, 46
  birth, 39
  Chicago and the Northwest, 39
  Diary of James K. Polk, 39
  Doctrine of Non-Intervention with Slavery in the Territories, 39
  as editor, 39, 46
  education, 39
  resignation, 42
Quinney, Austin E., *64*

radio, 44, 72–73, 95, 124
  WHA (radio), 72
  WLBL (radio), 72
Reed School, 100–102, *102*
  funding, 102
reenactments
  Civil War, 105
  vintage baseball, *105*
  War of 1812, 104
Remsen, Peter, 8

Ringling, Al, 81
Ringling, Alf, 81
Ringling, Charles, 81
Ringling, John, 81
Ringling, Otto, 81
Ringling Brothers Circus Train complex, 82
Ringling Brothers' winter quarters, 81, 115
Ringling Camel House, 82
Ringling Ring Barn, 82
Ripon, WI
    Little White Schoolhouse, 78
    local historical society, 25
Risking Everything: A Freedom Summer Reader (Edmonds), 74, 75
Roosevelt, Theodore, 26

Saint Augustine Church, 78
Sandburg, Carl, 68
Sauk County Historical Society, 78
Sawdust and Spangles: The Circus in Wisconsin (exhibit), 62
Schafer, Joseph, 42–48, 51, 127
    death, 48
    Memoirs of Jeremiah Curtin, 48
    The Winnebago-Horicon Basin, 48
Schwerner, Michael, 74
secretaries (WHS)
    corresponding, 5, 11, 19, 78, 127
    as director, 5, 127
    recording, 5
Seipp, Conrad
    Black Point Estate, 103, *103*
Sense of Community (exhibit), 93
Shake Rag Street, 86
shipwrecks, 117–118, *117*
Signers of the Declaration of Independence (exhibit), 62
Smith, Alice E., 90
Smith, James Morton, 90, 91, 127
social history, 2, 6–7, 9–10, 12, 14, 22, 56, 57–59, 81–88, 123
    Doomsday Project, 43, 48
social movements, 76
    civil rights movement, 73–76, *74, 75*
    organized labor, 2, 57–58, 73, 74
    Vietnam War, 73, 108, 112–113
Special Olympics of Wisconsin
    Cindy Bentley: Spirit of a Champion, 111

staff, 23, 36, 41, 42, 48–49, *53, 60,* 71,73, *73, 97, 106,* 119–120
    "Big Three," 24, 37, 41
    Library, 15, *15,* 22, 24, *25,* 45–46, *46,* 49, 72, 74, 89
    "Matriarchy," 24, 41
    Museum, 30–31, 32–33, *33,* 44, 49, 53, 59, 72, 79
    "the plumber from Kenosha," 54–55
    Wisconsin Historical Foundation, 119
    Wisconsin Historical Society Press, 63, 89
    women, 24, *25,* 37, 45–46, *46,* 48, 49, 72
State Agricultural Museum, 70
State Historical Society of Wisconsin, viii, 10. *See also* Wisconsin Historical Society
Stevens Point, WI
    WLBL (radio), 72
Stonefield, 65, 69–70, *69*
    State Agricultural Museum, 70
Stoughton, WI
    historic preservation, 116
Stoughton Opera House, *116*
superintendents. *See* directors

Taliesin, 115
Taste Traditions of Wisconsin program, 105
tax credit programs, 80, 115, 116–117, 118
technology, 27, 71, 95, 121
    book-lift, 28
    communications media, 44, 58, 59, 72–73, *73,* 95, 124
    computers, 34, 89, 95–98, 113, 116, 120, 124
    e-books, 113
    electricity, 27
    elevators, 28, *29*
    microfilm, 18, 48, 52, *53*
    radio, 44, 72–73, 95, 124
    telephones, 27
    television, 59, 72–73, *73,* 95, 106, 124
    typewriters, *25*
television, 59, 72–73, *73,* 95, 106, 124
    Antiques Road Show, 106
    Grandma's Attic, 72

Lori's Log Cabin, 72
Mysteries at the Museum, 106
TV Museum, 72
WHA-TV, 72, *73*
Wisconsin Public Television, 72, *73,*
    111–112
Wisconsin Vietnam War Stories, 112
Wisconsin Windows, 72
Thies, Donald, 112–113, 114
"Thinking Like a Historian" method,
    108
Thomasgard, Robert B., Jr., 127
Thomson, Vernon, *60*
Thwaites, Reuben Gold, 18–19, *18,*
    21–37, *21,* 40, 45, 48, 49, 51, 95,
    98, 123–124, 127
    annual reports, 26, 35–36
    as author, 25, 33
    birth, 18
    death, 36–37
    as editor, 33, 46
    Jesuit Relations, 33
    Journals of Lewis and Clark, 33
    as photographer, 25
Times (newspaper), 19
Titus, William A.
    WHS president, 51
treasurers (WHS), 5, 13
Trelawny, 86
Turner, Frederick Jackson, 23–24, 34,
    35, 37
TV Museum (television program), 72

underwater archaeology, 117–118, *117*
unions. *See* organized labor
United Artists collection, 59
US Army Corps of Engineers, 80
US National Park Service, 79
US Works Progress Administration, 48
University of Wisconsin, 8, 24–25, 37,
    48
    library, 28, 29, 46–47, 52, 63, 89
    Logmark Editions, 63
    Pail & Shovel Party, 99
    partnership with, 18, 23, 28, 29, 30,
        34, 44, 52, 58–59, 63, 89, 96–97
    pink flamingo, *99*
    Sterling Hall bombing, 106
    Wisconsin Center for Film and The-
        ater Research, 58–59

Urbanization and Industrialization (His-
    tory of Wisconsin series), 90

Van Schaick, Charles, 34
Vanderbilt, Paul, 59
Vernon County, WI
    La Farge Reservoir Project, 80
vice presidents (WHS), 3, 5
Vietnam War, 73, 108, 112–113
    Voices from Vietnam (Stevens), 112,
        114
    Wisconsin Vietnam War Stories (televi-
        sion program), 112
Villa Louis, 65–66, *67*
    Breakfast in a Victorian Kitchen, 104
    Carriage Classic, 104, *104*
    reenactments, 104
vintage baseball, *105*
Vogt, George L., 100, 127
Voices from Vietnam (Stevens), 112, *114*
volunteers, 89, 119, 120

Wade, Sylvanus
    Wade House, 66
Wade House, 66–68, *68,* 120–121
    Hearthside Dinner, 105
    Herrling Sawmill, 68
    reenactments, 105
    Wesley W. Jung Carriage House
        Museum, 68, 120–121
Walkway Gallery, 85
War, a New Era, and Depression (History
    of Wisconsin series), 90
War of 1812
    reenactments, 104
Water for Elephants (film), 106
Waupaca, WI
    Junior Historian Program, 61
Welsh, Iva, 24, 49
Wesley W. Jung Carriage House
    Museum, 68, 120–121
WHA (radio), 72
WHA-TV (television), 72, *73*
Wilson, Woodrow, 26
The Winnebago-Horicon Basin (Schafer),
    48
Wisconsin
    centennial, 61, 72
    constitutional conventions, 3, 8
    legislature, 10, 11, 14, 25, 27, 32, 35,

45, 47, 70, 78, 106, 115, 119
territorial legislature, 98, 100
Wisconsin Archaeological Society, 78
Wisconsin Architecture and History
    Inventory, 115–116
Wisconsin Archives Act, 32, 40
Wisconsin Center for Film and Theater
    Research, 58–59
    Hal Holbrook collection, 59
    Kirk Douglas collection, 59
    MTM Enterprises collection, 59
    United Artists collection, 59
Wisconsin Dells, WI, 101
    Bennett (H. H.) Studio, 100
Wisconsin Department of Natural Re-
    sources, 79
Wisconsin Federation of Women's
    Clubs, 78, 100
Wisconsin Highway Department, 78, 79
Wisconsin Historical Collections. See
    Collections
Wisconsin Historical Foundation,
    118–121
    Forward! The Campaign for the Wiscon-
        sin Historical Society, 119–121
    staff, 119
Wisconsin Historical Museum. See
    Museum
Wisconsin Historical Publications (Wis-
    consin Historical Society), 40. See
    also Collections
Wisconsin Historical Sites and Markers
    Committee, 57
Wisconsin Historical Society. See also
    Archives; directors; Library;
    Museum; staff
    attendance, 16, 18, 24, 53, 106, 107
    Board of Curators, 10, 41, 42, 51. See
        also executive committee
    charter, 9–10, 119
    communications, 40–41, 44, 72, 95
    constitution, 4, 10
    dues, 2, 5, 9, 10, 33, 119
    Editorial Division, 71
    and education, 23, 24, 36, 37, 42,
        44, 45, 52, 59–63, 60, 62, 80, 95,
        107–111, 109, 115, 124
    executive committee, 5, 9, 10, 13,
        32, 47. See also Board of Curators
    founding, 1, 3, 4–5
    funding, 2, 5, 10, 11, 14, 21, 22–23,
        27, 32, 33, 35, 43, 45, 47–48, 70,
        79, 97, 106, 119, 121, 123
    government relationship, 2, 10,
        14, 22–23, 26, 27, 32, 34, 35, 47,
        118–119
    headquarters, 3, 5–6, 11, 12, 14, 15,
        16, 22, 23, 26–32, 27, 28, 29, 30,
        35, 36, 46–47, 63, 71, 91–93, 91,
        96, 120, 124
    Historic Preservation Division, 80
    Junior Historian program, 59–60,
        60, 61–62, 108–110
    Manuscript Division, 46, 55, 71
    meetings, 3–5, 10
    membership, 2, 5, 9, 10, 22, 71, 118,
        119, 120, 123
    mission, 1, 4, 9–10, 24–25, 123
    Museum Department, 32
    name, viii, 10
    Office of Local History, 71
    officers, 3, 4, 4, 5, 9, 10, 11, 13, 19,
        51, 78, 127
    public relations, 22–23, 28, 44, 45,
        55, 63, 72, 90, 95
    publishing. See Wisconsin Historical
        Society Press
    reorganization, 4–5
    reputation, 24, 26, 32, 63, 123
    speakers, 4, 5, 9, 10, 25, 44, 46, 54,
        95, 105
    State Archaeologist, 71
    State Historic Preservation Office,
        79, 80, 115, 118
    State Register of Historic Places, 79,
        115
    visitors. See attendance
    volunteers, 89, 119, 120
Wisconsin Historical Society Library.
    See Library
Wisconsin Historical Society Press, 9,
    10, 11, 13–14, 18, 33–34, 37, 40,
    46, 48, 52, 63, 89–91, 107–108,
    111–114
    awards, 111
    Badger Biographies series, 108
    Collections, 13–14, 33–34, 40, 45–46
    Documentary History of the Ratification
        of the Constitution series, 90–91
    Doomsday Project, 43, 48

e-books, 113
History of Wisconsin series, 90
Logmark Editions, 63
magazines and newsletters, 39,
    40–41, *41*, 48, 52, 60–61, 89, 110,
    111, *112*
New Badger History series, 107–108
Places Along the Way series, 112,
    113
Proceedings, 33–34, 48
Spanish language editions, 108, *109*
staff, 63, 89
textbooks, 108, *109*
Wisconsin History Bulletin (magazine), 40
Wisconsin History Commission, 34–35
Wisconsin Idea, 24–25, 34, 37
Wisconsin Library Commission, 34
Wisconsin Magazine of History, 39,
    40–41, *41*, 48, 52, 89, 111, *112*
    awards, 111
Wisconsin Milk Marketing Board
    Creating Dairyland, 111
*Wisconsin: Nuestro Estado, Nuestra Histo-
    ria* (Malone et al), 108, *109*
Wisconsin: Our State, Our Story (Malone
    et al), 108, *109*
Wisconsin Public Television, 72, *73*,
    111–112
Wisconsin State Archaeologist, 71
Wisconsin State Historic Preservation
    Office, 79, 80, 115, 118
Wisconsin State Register of Historic
    Places, 79, 115

Wisconsin State Journal (newspaper),
    18, 19
Wisconsin Teacher Newsletter, 60
Wisconsin Vietnam War Stories (television
    program), 112
Wisconsin Volunteer Infantry
    commemorative roster, *13*
*Wisconsin: Wilderness, Territory, Frontier
    State* (exhibit), 62
Wisconsin Windows (television program),
    72
Wisconsin Women in the War (Hurn), 35
Wisconsin's Board for People with
    Developmental Disabilities
    Cindy Bentley: Spirit of a Champion,
    111
WLBL (radio), 72
Wolff, Kubly, and Hirsig hardware
    store, 93
women, 2, 123
    exhibit, 93
    staff, 24, *25*, 37, 45–46, *46*, 48, 49,
    72
    Wisconsin Women in the War (Hurn),
    35
World War I, 37, 42, 55
    War, a New Era, and Depression (His-
    tory of Wisconsin series), 90
World War II, 48, 51, 53, 54, 55
Worth, Charles Frederick, 45

Zane, Elizabeth
    papers in Draper Manuscripts, 18